Dickens' London

By
Francis Miltoun
Author of "The Cathedrals of Northern France"

With many Illustrations and Plans

Boston
L. C. Page & Company
MDCCCCIIII

All sublunary things of death partake!
What alteration does a cent'ry make!
Kings and Comedians all are mortal found,
Cæsar and Pinkethman are underground.
What's not destroyed by time's devouring hand?
Where's Troy, and where's the Maypole in the Strand?
Pease, cabbages, and turnips once grew where
Now stands New Bond Street and a newer square;
Such piles of buildings now rise up and down,
London itself seems going out of town.
          JAMES BRAMSTON, *The Art of Politicks.*

THE attempt is herein made to present in an informal manner such facts of historical, topographical, and literary moment as surrounded the localities especially identified with the life and work of Charles Dickens in the city of London, with naturally a not infrequent reference to such scenes and incidents as he was wont to incorporate in the results of his literary labours; believing that there are a considerable number of persons, travellers, lovers of Dickens, enthusiasts *et als.*, who might be glad of a work which should present within a single pair of covers a résumé of the facts concerning the subject matter indicated by the title of this book; to remind them in a way of what already exists to-day of the London Dickens knew, as well as of the changes which have taken place since the novelist's time.

To all such, then, the present work is offered, not necessarily as the last word or even as an exhaustive résumé, knowing full well the futility for any chronicler to attempt to do such a subject full justice within the confines of a moderate sized volume, where so many correlated facts of history and side lights of contemporary information are thrown upon the screen. The most that can be claimed is that every effort has been made to present a truthful, correct, and not unduly sentimental account of the sights and scenes of London connected with the life of Charles Dickens.

In Praise of London

"The inhabitants of St. James', notwithstanding they live under the same laws and speak the same language, are as a people distinct from those who live in the 'City.'"

Addison.

"If you wish to have a just notion of the magnitude of the City you must not be satisfied with its streets and squares, but must survey the innumerable little lanes and courts."

Johnson.

"I have often amused myself with thinking how different a place London is to different people."

Boswell.

"I had rather be Countess of Puddle-Dock (in London) than Queen of Sussex."

Shadwell.

"London . . . a place where next-door neighbours do not know one another."

Fielding.

"London . . . where all people under thirty find so much amusement."

Gray.

"Dull as London is in summer, there is always more company in it than in any other one place."

Walpole.

"London! Opulent, enlarged, and still — increasing London!"

Cowper.

"What is London?"

Burke.

"I began to study a map of London . . . the river is of no assistance to a stranger in finding his way."

Southey.

Contents

List of Illustrations

List of Illustrations

Dickens' London

INTRODUCTION

*T*HIS book is for the lover of Dickens and
of London, alike. The former without
the memory of the latter would indeed be
wanting, and likewise the reverse would be the case.
London, its life and its stones, has ever been immortalized by authors and artists, but more than
all else, the city has been a part of the very life and
inspiration of those who have limned its virtues,
its joys, and its sorrows, — from the days of blithe
Dan Chaucer to those of the latest west-end society
novelist.

London, as has been truly said, is a "mighty
mingling," and no one has breathed more than
Dickens the spirit of its constantly shifting and
glimmering world of passion and poverty.

The typical Londoner of to-day — as in the early
Victorian period of which Dickens mostly wrote

— is a species quite apart from the resident of any other urban community throughout the world. Since the spell which is recorded as first having fallen upon the ear of Whittington, the sound of Bow Bells is the only true and harmonious ring which, to the ears of the real cockney, recalls all that is most loved in the gamut of his sentiments.

It is perhaps not possible to arrange the contents of a book of the purport of this volume in true chronological, or even topographical, order. The first, because of the necessitous moving about, hither and then thither, — the second, because of the fact that the very aspect of the features of the city are constantly under a more or less rapid process of evolution, which is altering all things but the points of the compass and the relative position of St. Paul's and Westminster Abbey. Between these two guide-posts is a mighty maze of streets, ever changing as to its life and topography.

Hungerford Market and Hungerford Stairs have disappeared, beside which was the blacking factory, wherein the novelist's first bitter experiences of London life were felt, — amid a wretchedness only too apparent, when one reads of the miserable days which fell upon the lad at this time, — the market itself being replaced by the huge Charing Cross Railway Station, in itself no architectural improvement, it may be inferred, while the "crazy old houses and wharves" which fronted the river have likewise been dissipated by the march of improvement, which left in its wake the glorious, though little used, Victoria Embankment, one of the few really fine modern thoroughfares of a great city.

Eastward again Furnival's Inn, where Pickwick was written, has fallen at the hands of the housebreaker.

The office of the old *Monthly Magazine* is no more, its very doorway and letter-box — "wherein was dropped stealthily one night" the precious manuscript of "Pickwick" — being now in the possession of an ardent Dickens collector, having been removed from its former site in Johnson's Court in Fleet Street at the time the former edifice was pulled down.

Across the river historic and sordid Marshalsea, where the elder Dickens was incarcerated for debt, has been dissipated in air; even its walls are not visible to-day, if they even exist, and a modern park — though it is mostly made up of flagstones — stands in its place as a moral, healthful, and politic force of the neighbourhood.

With the scenes and localities identified with the plots and characters of the novels the same cleaning up process has gone on, one or another shrine being from time to time gutted, pulled to pieces, or removed. On the other hand, doubtless much that existed in the fancy, or real thought, of the author still remains, as the door-knocker of No. 8 Craven Street, Strand, the conjectured original of which is described in the "Christmas Carol," which appeared to the luckless Scrooge as "not a knocker but Marley's face;" or the Spaniards Inn on Hampstead Heath described in the XLVI. Chapter of Pickwick, which stands to-day but little, if any, changed since that time.

For the literary life of the day which is reflected by the mere memory of the names of such of Dickens' contemporaries in art and letters, as Mark Lemon, W. H. Wills, Wilkie Collins, Cruikshank, "Phiz," Forster Blanchard, Jerrold, Maclise, Fox, Dyce, and Stanfield, one can only resort to a history of mid or early Victorian literature to realize the same to the full. Such is not the scheme of this book, but that London, — the city, — its surroundings, its lights and shadows, its topography, and its history, rather, is to be followed in a sequence of co-related events presented with as great a degree of cohesion and attractive arrangement as will be thought to be commensurate and pertinent to the subject. Formerly, when London was a "snug city," authors more readily confined their incomings

MRS. TULKINGHORN'S HOUSE.

NO. 8 CRAVEN STREET, STRAND.

and outgoings to a comparatively small area. To-day " the city " is a term only synonymous with a restricted region which gathers around the financial centre, while the cabalistic letters (meaning little or nothing to the stranger within the gates), E. C., safely comprehend a region which not only includes " *the city*," but extends as far westward as Temple Bar, and thus covers, if we except the lapping over into the streets leading from the Strand, practically the whole of the " Highway of Letters " of Doctor Johnson's time.

A novelist to-day, and even so in Dickens' time, did not — nay could not — give birth to a character which could be truly said to represent the complex London type. The environment of the lower classes — the east end and the Boro' — is ever redolent of him, and he of it. The lower-middle or upper-lower class is best defined by that individual's predilection for the " good old Strand; " while as the scale rises through the petty states of Suburbia to the luxuries of Mayfair or Belgravia, — or to define one locality more precisely, Park Lane, — we have all the ingredients with which the novelist constructs his stories, be they of the nether world, or the " *hupper suckles.*" Few have there been who have essayed both. And now the suburbs are breeding their own school of novelists. Possibly it is the residents of those communities who demand a special brand of fiction, as they do of coals, paraffine, and boot-polish.

At any rate the London that Dickens knew clung somewhat to Wordsworth's happy description written but a half century before:

" Silent, bare,
 Ships, towers, domes, theatres, and temples lie,
 Open unto the fields and to the sky,"

whereas to-day, as some " New Zealander " from the back blocks has said: " *These Londoners they never seen no sun.*" And thus it is that the scale runs from grave to gay, from poverty to purse full, and ever London, — the London of the past as well as the present, of Grub Street as well as Grosvenor Square. The centre of the world's literary activities, where, if somewhat conventional as to the acceptation of the new idea in many of the marts of trade, it is ever prolific in the launching of some new thing in literary fashions.

At least it is true that London still merits the eulogistic lines penned not many years gone by by a certain minor poet:

" *Ah, London ! London !   Our delight,*
Great flower that opens but at night,
Great city of the Midnight Sun,
Whose day begins when day is done."

It is said of the industrious and ingenious American that he demands to be "shown things," and if his cicerone is not sufficiently painstaking he will play the game after his own fashion, which usually results in his getting into all sorts of unheard-of places, and seeing and learning things which your native has never suspected to previously have existed. All honour then to such an indefatigable species of the *genus homo.*

Nothing has the peculiar charm of old houses for the seeker after knowledge. To see them, and to know them, is to know their environment, — and so it is with London, — and then, and then only, can one say truly — in the words of Johnson — that they have "seen and are astonished."

A great mass of the raw material from which English history is written is contained in parochial record books and registers, and if this were the only source available the fund of information concerning the particular section of mid-London with which Dickens was mostly identified — the parishes of St. Bride's, St. Mary's-le-Strand, St. Dunstan's, St. Clement's-Danes, and St. Giles — would furnish a well-nigh inexhaustible store of old-time lore. For a fact, however, the activities of the nineteenth century alone, to particularize an era, in the " Highway of Letters " and the contiguous streets lying round about, have formed the subject of many a big book quite by itself. When one comes to still further approximate a date the task is none the less formidable; hence it were hardly possible to more than limn herein a sort of fleeting itinerary among the sights and scenes which once existed, and point out where, if possible, are the differences that exist to-day. Doctor Johnson's "walk down Fleet Street" — if taken at the present day — would at least be productive of many surprises, whether pleasant ones or not the reader may adduce for himself, though doubtless the learned doctor would still chant the praises of the city — in that voice which we infer was none too melodious:

" Oh, in town let me live, then in town let me die,
For in truth I can't relish the country ; not I."

Within the last decade certain changes have taken place in this thoroughfare which might be expected to make it unrecognizable to those of a former generation who may have known it well. Improvements for the better, or the worse, have rapidly taken place; until now there is, in truth, somewhat of an approach to a wide thoroughfare leading from Westminster to the city. But during the process something akin to a holocaust has taken place, to consider only the landmarks and shrines which have disappeared, — the last as these lines are being written, being Clifford's Inn, — while Mrs. Tulkinghorn's house in Lincoln's Inn Fields, redolent of Dickens and Forster, his biographer, is doomed, as also the *Good Words* offices in Wellington Street, where Dickens spent so much of his time in the later years of his life. The famous " Gaiety " is about to be pulled down, and the " old Globe " has already gone from this street of taverns, as well as of letters, or, as one picturesque writer has called it, " the nursing mother of English literature."

THE LONDON DICKENS KNEW

*T*HE father of Charles Dickens was for a time previous to the birth of the novelist a clerk in the Navy Pay Office, then in Somerset House, which stands hard by the present Waterloo Bridge, in the very heart of London, where Charles Dickens grew to manhood in later years.

From this snug berth Dickens, senior, was transferred to Portsmouth, where, at No. 387 Commercial Road, in Portsea, on the 7th February, 1812, Charles Dickens was born.

Four years later the family removed to Chatham, near Rochester, and here the boy Charles received his first schooling.

From Chatham the family again removed, this time to London, where the son, now having arrived at the age of eleven, became a part and parcel of that life which he afterward depicted so naturally and successfully in the novels.

Here he met with the early struggles with grim

poverty and privation, — brought about by the vicissitudes which befell the family, — which proved so good a school for his future career as a historian of the people. His was the one voice which spoke with authoritativeness, and aroused that interest in the nether world which up to that time had slumbered.

The miseries of his early struggles with bread-winning in Warren's Blacking Factory, — in association with one Fagin, who afterward took on immortalization at the novelist's hands, — for a weekly wage of but six shillings per week, is an old and realistic fact which all biographers and most makers of guide-books have worn nearly threadbare.

That the family were sore put in order to keep their home together, first in Camden Town and later in Gower Street, North, is only too apparent. The culmination came when the elder Dickens was thrown into Marshalsea Prison for debt, and the family removed thither, to Lant Street, near by, in order to be near the head of the family.

This is a sufficiently harrowing sequence of events to allow it to be left to the biographers to deal with them to the full. Here the author glosses it over as a mere detail; one of those indissoluble links which connects the name of Dickens with the life of London among the lower and middle classes during the Victorian era.

An incident in " David Copperfield," which Dickens has told us was real, so far as he himself was concerned, must have occurred about this period. The reference is to the visit to " Ye Olde Red Lion " at the corner of Derby Street, Parliament Street, near Westminster Bridge, which house has only recently disappeared. He has stated that it was an actual experience of his own childhood, and how, being such a little fellow, the landlord, instead of drawing the ale, called his wife, who gave the boy a motherly kiss.

The incident as recounted in " David Copperfield " called also for a glass of ale, and reads not unlike:

" I remember one hot evening I went into the bar of a public-house, and said to the landlord: ' What is your best — your *very best* ale a glass?' For it was a special occasion. I don't know what. It may have been my birthday. ' Twopence-halfpenny,' says the landlord, ' is the price of the Genuine Stunning Ale.' ' Then,' says I, producing the money, ' just draw me a glass of the Genuine Stunning, if you please, with a good head to it.' "

After a time his father left the Navy Pay Office and entered journalism. The son was clerking, meanwhile, in a solicitor's office, — that of Edward Blackmore, — first in Lincoln's Inn, and subsequently in Gray's Inn. A diary of the author was recently sold by auction, containing as its first entry, " 13s 6d for one week's salary." Here Dickens acquired that proficiency in making mental memoranda of his environment, and of the manners and customs of lawyers and their clerks, which afterward found so vivid expression in " Pickwick."

By this time the father's financial worries had ceased, or at least made for the better. He had entered the realms of journalism and became a Parliamentary reporter, which it is to be presumed developed a craving on the part of Charles for a similar occupation; when following in his father's footsteps, he succeeded, after having learned Gurney's system of shorthand, in obtaining an appointment as a reporter in the press gallery of the House of Commons (the plans for the new Parliament buildings were just then taking shape), where he was afterward acknowledged as being one of the most skilful and accomplished shorthand reporters in the galleries of that unconventional, if deliberate, body, which even in those days, though often counting as members a group of leading statesmen, perhaps ranking above those of the present day, was ever a democratic though " faithful " parliamentary body.

In 1834 the old Houses of Parliament were

burned, and with the remains of St. Stephen's Hall the new structure grew up according to the plan presented herein, which is taken from a contemporary print.

At the end of the Parliamentary session of 1836 Dickens closed his engagement in the Reporters' Gallery, a circumstance which he recounts thus in Copperfield, which may be presumed to be somewhat of autobiography:

" I had been writing in the newspapers and elsewhere so prosperously that when my new success was achieved I considered myself reasonably entitled to escape from the dreary debates. One joyful night, therefore, I noted down the music of the Parliamentary bagpipes for the last time, and I have never heard it since." (" David Copperfield," Chap. XLVIII.)

Again, in the same work, the novelist gives us some account of the effort which he put into the production of " Pickwick." " I laboured hard " — said he — " at my book, without allowing it to interfere with the punctual discharge of my newspaper duties, and it came out and was very successful. I was not stunned by the praise which sounded in my ears, notwithstanding that I was keenly alive to it. For this reason I retained my modesty in very self-respect; and the more praise I got the

CHARLES DICKENS WAS PARLIAMENTARY RE-
PORTER ON THIS PAPER.

more I tried to deserve." ("David Copperfield,"
Chap. XLVIII.)

From this point onward in the career of Charles
Dickens, he was well into the maelstrom of the life
of letters with which he was in the future to be so
gloriously identified; and from this point forward,
also, the context of these pages is to be more allied
with the personality (if one may be permitted to so
use the word) of the environment which surrounded
the life and works of the novelist, than with the
details of that life itself.

In reality, it was in 1833, when Dickens had just
attained his majority, that he first made the plunge
into the literary whirlpool. He himself has related
how one evening at twilight he "had stealthily entered a dim court" (Johnson's Court, Fleet Street,
not, as is popularly supposed, named for Doctor
Johnson, though inhabited by him in 1766, from
whence he removed in the same year to Bolt Court,
still keeping to his beloved Fleet Street), and
through an oaken doorway, with a yawning letter-
box, there fell the MS. of a sketch entitled "A
Dinner at Poplar Walk," afterward renamed "Mr.
Minns and His Cousin." These were the offices
of the old *Monthly Magazine* now defunct. Here
the article duly appeared as one of the "Sketches
by Boz." In the preface to an edition of "Pick-

wick," published in 1847, Dickens describes the incident sufficiently graphically for one to realize, to its fullest extent, with what pangs, and hopes, and fears his trembling hand deposited the first of the children of his brain; a foundling upon the doorstep where it is to be feared so many former and later orphans were, if not actually deserted, abandoned to their fate.

These were parlous times in Grub Street; in the days when the art of letters, though undeniably prolific, was not productive of an income which would assure even a practised hand freedom from care and want. Within a half-mile on either side of this blind alley leading off Fleet Street, from Ludgate Hill on the east — redolent of memories of the Fleet, its Prison, and its " Marriages " — to Somerset House on the west, is that unknown land, that *terra incognita*, whereon so many ships of song are stranded, or what is more, lost to oblivion which is blacker than darkness itself.

In January, 1837, while still turning out " Pickwick " in monthly parts, Dickens was offered the editorship of the already famous *Bentley's Magazine*, which he accepted, and also undertook to write " Oliver Twist " for the same periodical.

In March, of the same year, the three rooms at Furnival's Inn presumably having become crowded beyond comfort, he removed with his wife to his former lodgings at Chalk, where the couple had spent their honeymoon, and where in the following year their son Charles was born. What memories are conjured up of the past and, it is to be hoped, of future greatness by those who, in taking their walks abroad, find themselves within the confines of the parish of St. Bride's, with its church built by Wren shortly after the great fire, and its queer pointed steeple, like a series of superimposed tabourets overtopped with a needle-like spire?

Here the brazen chimes ring out to all and sundry of the world of journalism and letters, whose vocations are carried on within its sound, the waking and sleeping hours alike. True! there are no sleeping hours in Fleet Street; night is like unto day, and except for the absence of the omnibuses, and crowds of hurrying throngs of city men and solicitors and barristers, the faces of those you meet at night are in no way unlike the same that are seen during the hours in which the sun is supposed to shine in London, but which — for at least five months of the year — mostly doesn't.

Old St. Bride's, destroyed by the great fire of London in the seventeenth century, sheltered the remains of Sackville, who died in 1608, and the

printer, Wynken de Worde, and of Lovelace (1658).
To-day in the present structure the visitor may see
the tomb of Richardson, the author of " Clarissa
Harlow," who lived in Salisbury Square, another
near-by centre of literary activity. In the adjacent
churchyard formerly stood a house in which Milton
for a time resided. In later times it has been mostly
called to the minds of lion hunters as being the
living of the Reverend E. C. Hawkins, the father
of our most successful and famed epigrammatic
novelist, — Mr. Anthony Hope Hawkins.

Equally reminiscent, and linked with a literary
past in that close binding and indissoluble fashion
which is only found in the great world of London,
are such place names as Bolt Court, where Johnson
spent the last years of his life (1776-1784), Wine
Office Court, in which is still situated the ancient
hostelry, "The Cheshire Cheese," where all good
Americans repair to sit, if possible, in the chair
which was once graced (?) by the presence of the
garrulous doctor, or to buy alleged pewter tankards,
which it is confidently asserted are a modern
" Brummagem " product " made to sell." Gough
Square at the top of Wine Office Court is where
Johnson conceived and completed his famous dictionary. Bouverie Street (is this, by the way, a
corruption or a variant of the Dutch word *Bouerie*

which New Yorkers know so well?), across the way, leads toward the river where once the Carmelite friary (White Friars) formerly stood, and to a region which Scott has made famous in " Nigel " as " Alsatia." Fetter Lane, and Great and Little New Streets, leading therefrom, are musty with a literary or at least journalistic atmosphere. Here Izaak Walton, the gentle angler, lived while engaged in the vocation of hosier at the corner of Chancery Lane.

At the corner of Bouverie Street are the *Punch* offices, to which mirthful publication Dickens made but one contribution, — and that was never published. Further adown the street is still the building which gave shelter to the famous dinners of the round-table when all the wits of *Punch* met and dined together, frequently during the London season.

In Mitre Court, until recently, stood the old tavern which had, in its palmier if not balmier days, been frequently the meeting-place of Johnson, Goldsmith, and Boswell; while but a short distance away we are well within the confines of the Temple which not only sheltered and fostered the law, but literature as well.

An incident which shows Dickens' sympathy with the literary life of the day was in 1854, when

the great-grandson of the man who has given so
much to all ages of Englishmen, — De Foe, — was
made happy with a relief of £2 a month. Dickens
was (as might have been expected) amongst the
most liberal subscribers to the little fund. If everybody who has derived delight from the perusal of
" Robinson Crusoe " had but contributed a single
farthing to his descendant, that descendant would
become a wealthy man. When De Foe was asked
what he knew of his great ancestor's writings, he
answered (though doubtless without any inten-
tional comment on his ancestor's reputation) that
in his happier days he had several of De Foe's
works; but that he never could keep a copy of
" Robinson Crusoe; " " there were so many bor-
rowers of the book in Hungerford Market alone."
Charles Knight, the publisher and antiquarian, insti-
tuted the fund, and the money was raised by him
chiefly among literary men.

The most sentimental and picturesque interest
attaches itself to the extensive series of buildings
on the south side of Fleet Street, familiarly known
as the Temple. Here Goldsmith is buried beside the
curious and interesting Temple Church. The other
of the four great Inns of Court are Lincoln's Inn
in Chancery Lane and Gray's Inn in Holborn. Allied with the four great inns were the more or less

subsidiary Inns of Chancery, all situated in the immediate neighbourhood, one of which, at least, being intimately associated with Dickens' life in London — Furnival's Inn, which, with Thavie's Inn, was attached to Lincoln's Inn. Here Dickens lived in 1835 at No. 15, and here also he lived subsequent to his marriage with Catherine Hogarth in the following year. It was at this time that the first number of "Pickwick" was written and published. The building itself was pulled down sometime during the past few years.

Comprising several squares and rows, what is commonly referred to as the Temple, belongs to the members of two societies, the Inner and Middle Temple, consisting of "benchers," barristers, and students. This famous old place, taken in its completeness, was, in 1184, the metropolitan residence of the Knights Templars, who held it until their downfall in 1313; soon afterward it was occupied by students of the law; and in 1608 James I. presented the entire group of structures to the "benchers" of the two societies, who have ever since been the absolute owners. The entrance to Inner Temple, from Fleet Street, is nothing more than a mere gateway; the entrance to Middle Temple is more pretentious, and was designed by Sir Christopher Wren.

Here in the heart of the great world of London exists, as in no other city on the globe, a quiet and leafy suburb, peopled only by those whose vocation is not of the commonalty. Its very environment is inspiring to great thoughts and deeds, and small wonder it is that so many master minds have first received their stimulus amid the shady walks and rather gloomy buildings of the Temple.

True it is that they are gloomy, on the outside at least, — dull brick rows with gravelled or flagged courtyards, but possessing withal a geniality which many more glaring and modern surroundings utterly lack.

The stranger, for sightseeing, and the general public, to take advantage of a short cut to the river, throng its walks during the busy hours around noontime. All sorts and conditions of men hurry busily along in a never-ending stream, but most to be remarked is the staid and earnest jurist, his managing clerk, or the aspiring bencher, as his duties compel him to traverse this truly hallowed ground.

By nightfall the atmosphere and associations of the entire Temple take on, if possible, a more quiet and somnolescent air than by day. It must, if report be true, be like a long-deserted city in the small hours of the night. A group of chambers, called rather con-

temptuously Paper Buildings, is near the river and
is a good example of revived Elizabethan architecture. A new Inner Temple Hall was formally
opened in 1870, by the Princess Louise. In October,
1861, when the Prince of Wales was elected a
bencher of the Middle Temple, the new Library was
formally opened. The Temple Church, as seen from
the river, with its circular termination, like nothing
else in the world except Charlemagne's church at
Aix la Chapelle, is one of the most interesting
churches in London. All the main parts of the
structure are as old as the time of the Knights
Templars; but restorations of the middle nineteenth
century, when the munificent sum of £70,000 was
spent, are in no small way responsible for its many
visible attributes which previously had sadly fallen
to decay. There are two portions, the Round
Church and the Choir, the one nearly 700 years
old and the other more than 600. The chief distinguishing features of the interior are the monumental effigies, the original sculptured heads in the
Round Church, the triforium, and the fittings of
the Choir. The north side of the church has been
opened out by the removal of the adjoining buildings where, in the churchyard, is the grave of Oliver
Goldsmith, who died in chambers (since pulled
down) in Brick Court. The Temple Gardens,

fronting the river, are laid out as extensive shrub and tree-bordered lawns, which are generously thrown open to the public in the summer. A more charming sylvan retreat, there is not in any city in the world.

In the good old times, legal education and hospitality went hand in hand, and the halls of the different Inns of Court were, for several centuries, a kind of university for the education of advocates, subject to this arrangement. The benchers and readers, being the superiors of each house, occupied, on public occasions of ceremony, the upper end of the hall, which was raised on a daïs, and separated from the rest of the building by a *bar*. The next in degree were the *utter* barristers, who, after they had attained a certain standing, were called from the body of the hall to the bar (that is, to the first place outside the bar), for the purpose of taking a principal part in the mootings or exercises of the house; and hence they probably derived the name of *utter* or outer barristers. The other members of the inn, consisting of students of the law under the degree of *utter* barristers, took their places nearer to the centre of the hall, and farther from the bar, and, from this manner of distribution, appear to have been called inner barristers. The distinction between *utter* and inner barristers is, at the present day, wholly abolished; the former being called barristers generally, and the latter falling under the denomination of students; but the phrase "called to the bar" still holds and is recognized throughout the English-speaking world.

The general rule, as to qualification, in all the Inns of Court, is, that a person, in order to entitle himself to be called to the bar, must be twenty-one years of age, have kept *twelve terms,* and have been for five, or three years, at least, a member of the society. The keeping of terms includes dining a certain number of times in the hall, and hence the pleasantry of *eating the way to the bar;* the preparatory studies being now private. Of the great business of refection, the engraving herewith shows the most dignified scene — the Benchers' Dinner; the benchers, or "antients," as they were formerly called, being the governors of the inn, at the Temple called the Parliament. The Middle Temple hall surpasses the halls of the other societies in size and splendour. Begun in 1562, and finished about ten years afterward, it is 100 feet long, 40 feet wide, and upwards of 60 feet in height. The roof and panels are finely decorated, and the screen at the lower end is beautifully carved. There are a few good pictures: amongst others, one of Charles I.

on horseback, by Vandyke; also portraits of Charles II., Queen Anne, George I., and George II.

Lincoln's Inn was once the property of Henry De Lacy, Earl of Lincoln. It became an Inn of Court in 1310. The New Hall and Library, a handsome structure after the Tudor style, was opened in 1845. The Chapel was built in 1621-23, by Inigo Jones, who laid out the large garden in Lincoln's Inn Fields, close by, in 1620. Lord William Russell was beheaded here in 1683. In Lincoln's Inn are the Chancery and Equity Courts. Lincoln's Inn vied with the Temple in the masques and revels of the time of James I.

Gray's Inn, nearly opposite the north end of Chancery Lane, once belonged to the Lords Gray of Wilton. Most of its buildings — except its hall, with its black oak roof — are of comparatively modern date. In Gray's Inn lived the great Lord Bacon, a tree planted by whom, in the quaint old garden of the Inn, could, in Dickens' time, yet be seen — propped up by iron stays. To-day a diligent search and inquiry does not indicate its whereabouts, which is another manifestation of the rapidity of the age in which we live.

The nine Inns of Chancery allied with the four Inns of Court, the Inner and Middle Temple, Lincoln's Inn and Gray's Inn, are Clifford's Inn, Clement's Inn, Lyons' Inn, New Inn, Furnival's Inn, Thavie's Inn, Sergeant's Inn, Staple Inn, and Barnard's Inn, all of which were standing in Dickens' day, but of which only Staple Inn and Sergeant's Inn have endured, Clement's Inn having only recently (1903) succumbed to the house-breaker.

Staple Inn, in Holborn, "the fayrest inne of Chancerie," is one of the quaintest, quietest, and most interesting corners of mediæval London left to us.

Nathaniel Hawthorne, describing his first wanderings in London, said, "I went astray in Holborn through an arched entrance over which was Staple Inn, and here likewise seemed to be offices; but in a court opening inwards from this, there was a surrounding seclusion of quiet dwelling-houses, with beautiful green shrubbery and grass-plots in the court and a great many sunflowers in full bloom. The windows were open, it was a lovely summer afternoon, and I had a sense that bees were humming in the court." Many more years have passed over the old corner since Hawthorne's visit, but still it retains its ancient charm, and still the visitor is struck by the rapid change from the hurrying stream of Holborn's traffic to this haunt of ancient peace about which Mr. Worsfold writes with pardonable enthusiasm.

With a history traceable backward for many centuries, Staple Inn was at first associated in the middle ages with the dealing in the " staple commodity " of wool, to use Lord Chief Justice Coke's words, but about the fifteenth century the wool merchants gave way to the wearers of woollen " stuff," and their old haunt became one of the Inns of Chancery — the Staple Inn of the lawyers — perpetuating its origin in its insignia, a bale of wool. For many years the connection of the Inn with the Law was little beyond a nominal one, and in 1884 the great change came, and the haunt of merchants, the old educational establishment for lawyers, passed from the hands of " The Principal, Ancients and Juniors of the Honourable Society of Staple Inn," to those of a big insurance society, while the fine old hall became the headquarters of the Institute of Actuaries.

True it is, that perhaps no area of the earth's surface, of say a mile square, has a tithe of the varied literary association of the neighbourhood lying in the immediate vicinity of the Temple, the birthplace of Lamb, the home of Fielding, and the grave of Goldsmith.

Shoe Lane, Fleet Street, is still haunted by the memory of the boy Chatterton, and Will's Coffee House, the resort of wits and literary lights of former days, vies with Royal Palaces as an attraction for those who would worship at the shrines of a bygone age, — a process which has been made the easier of late, now that the paternal Society of Arts has taken upon itself to appropriately mark, by means of a memorial tablet, many of these localities, of which all mention is often omitted from the guide-books. Often the actual houses themselves have disappeared, and it may be questioned if it were not better that in some instances a tablet commemorating a home or haunt of some notability were not omitted. Still if the accompanying inscription is only sufficiently explicit, the act is a worthy one, and truth to tell, a work that is well performed in London.

Suburban London, too, in a way, may well come within the scope of the passion of any lover of material things which have at one time or another been a part and parcel of the lives of great men. And so, coupled with literary associations, we have the more or less imaginary " Bell " at Edmonton to remind us of Cowper, of many houses and scenes identified with Carlyle, at Chelsea; of the poet Thompson, of Gainsborough, and a round score of celebrities who have been closely identified with Richmond, — and yet others as great, reminiscent of Pepys, Addison, Steele, Thackeray and the whole

noble band of chroniclers, essayists, and diarists of
the seventeenth, eighteenth and nineteenth centuries.

The "houses of entertainment" — as the Geor-
gian novelist was pleased to refer to inns and taverns
— had in Dickens' day not departed greatly from
their original status. Referring solely to those
coaching and posting-houses situated at a greater
or lesser distance from the centre of town, — on
the main roads running therefrom, and those city
establishments comprehended strictly under the
head of taverns, — which were more particularly
places of refreshment for mankind of the genus
male. These two classes were, and are, quite distinct from the later-day *caravanserai* known as
hotels, and as such performed vastly different functions.

To be sure, all life and movement of the early
nineteenth century, and for a couple of hundred
years before, had a great deal to do with inns and
taverns.

From Chaucer's famous "Tabard," where —

> "*In Southwark at the Tabard as I lay*
> *Ready to wenden on my pilgrimage,*"

to "The Bull," at Rochester, whose courtyard is
still as described by Dickens, and the somewhat
mythical "Maypole" of "Barnaby Rudge," is a

far cry, though it would appear that the kind of cheer and accommodation varies to a much lesser degree than might be supposed. Certainly the demand for brevity and the luxuriousness of the later years of the nineteenth century, and even to some extent during Dickens' time, with the innovation of railway travel, gas-lamps, the telegraph, and what not, was making an entirely new set of conditions and demands.

The old "Tabard" of Chaucer's day is no more, though an antiquary of 1840 has attempted to construct what it may have been out of the "Talbot" of that day, which stood in the ancient High Street of Southwark, just across London Bridge, where, said the annalist Stow, "there were so many fair inns for receipt of travellers," — the rivals of the Boar's Heads and Mermaids of another generation.

Of the actual Dickens' inns, perhaps none is more vividly impressed on the imagination than that of the "Maypole," that fantastic structure of "Barnaby Rudge," the original of which is the "King's Head" at Chigwell on the borders of Epping Forest. It was here that Mr. Willet sat in his accustomed place, "his eyes on the eternal boiler." "Before he had got his ideas into focus, he had stared at the plebeian utensil quite twenty minutes," — all of which indicates the minutiæ and

precision of Dickens' observations. This actual
copper, vouched for by several documents of attestation, with an old chair which formerly stood in
the Chester Room of the "Maypole," is to-day in
the possession of Mr. Bransby Williams, of London, an ardent enthusiast of all matters in connection with Dickens and his stories.

Of the *Pickwickian Inns*, the "White Horse"
at Ipswich — "the overgrown tavern" to which
Mr. Pickwick journeyed by the London Coach —
is something of tangible reality, and doubtless little
changed to this day; the same being equally true of
"The Leather Bottle" at Cobham. The old
"White Hart" in the Borough High Street, the
scene of the first meeting of Mr. Pickwick and
Weller, was demolished in 1889. Not so the
"Magpie and Stump," — that referred to in "Pickwick" as being in the vicinity of the Clare Market,
and "closely approximating to the back of the
'New Inn.'" This seems to have been of an imaginary character in nomenclature, at least, though
it is like enough that some neighbourhood hostelry — or, as it is further referred to, as being
what the ordinary person would call a "low public-house" — was in mind.

The old "Fountain Inn" of the Minories, referred
to in "Oliver Twist," and the "little inn" ("The

Sun ") at Canterbury, where the Micawbers lodged, and the " White Hart " at Hook, — or more probably its predecessor of the same name, — visited by the Pickwickians en route to Rochester, — were realities in every sense of the word, and show once again the blending of truth and fiction which was so remarkable in the novels, and which indicates so strongly the tendency of Dickens to make every possible use of accessories, sights, and scenes, with which, at one time or another, he had been acquainted.

The " Saracen's Head " at Snow Hill, — a real thing in Dickens' day, — where the impetuous Squeers put up during his visits to London, has disappeared. It was pulled down when the Holborn Viaduct was built in 1869, and the existing house of the same name in no way merits the genial regard which is often bestowed upon it, in that it is but an ordinary London " *Pub* " which does not even occupy the same site as its predecessor.

" The Spaniards," where foregathered the No-Popery rioters, on Hampstead Heath, remains much as of yore; certainly it has not changed to any noticeable degree since Mrs. Bardell, *et als.,* repaired hither in the Hampstead stage for their celebrated tea-party, as recounted in " Pickwick."

The very term *Pickwickian Inns* inspires rumination and imagination to a high degree. Remembrance is all very well, but there is a sturdy reality about most of the inns of which Dickens wrote. Thus the enthusiast may, if he so wish, in some cases, become a partaker of the same sort of comfort as did Dickens in his own time, or at least, amid the same surroundings; though it is to be feared that New Zealand mutton and Argentine beef have usurped the place in the larder formerly occupied by the "primest Scotch" and the juiciest "Southdown."

It is said there are twenty-five inns mentioned in "Pickwick" alone; the writer has never been able to count up but twenty-two: still the assertion may be correct; he leaves it to the curious to verify. Certainly such well revered names as the "Golden Cross," "The Bull," at Rochester, which, above all other localities drawn in "Pickwick," has the liveliest associations, "The Leather Bottle," "The Magpie and Stump," "The Marquis of Granby," "The Blue Boar," "The White Horse Cellars" in Piccadilly, and "The Great White Horse" at Ipswich are for ever branded upon the memory. The following half-dozen will perhaps be best recalled: "The Old White Hart" in the Borough High Street; "The George and Vulture," Mr. Pickwick's own favourite: "The Golden Cross," remi-

niscent of Dickens' own personality as well; " The
White Horse Cellars," the starting-place of the
Ipswich Coach; " Osborne's Hotel " in the Adelphi,
still occupied as a rather shabby sort of hostelry,
though the name has gone; " Jack Straw's Castle,"
where " Boz " and his friend Forster so often en-
joyed that " shoemaker's holiday; " and lastly,
" The Spaniards " at Hampstead. A description of
one, as it is to-day, must suffice here.

" The Golden Cross," which stands opposite Charing Cross Railway Station, with its floriated gilt
crosses usually brightly burnished, and the entire
edifice resplendent in new paint.

There is still, however, something of the air of
the conservatism of a former day, if only in the
manner of building, which in the present case fur-
thers the suggestion that the ways of the modern
architect — striving for new and wonderful con-
structive methods — were unknown when the walls
of this old hostelry were put up.

Its courtyard has disappeared, or rather has been
incorporated into a sort of warehouse or stable for
a parcels delivery company, and the neighbourhood
round about has somewhat changed since the days
of " Copperfield " and " Pickwick." The Charing
Cross Railway Station has come upon the scene,
replacing old Hungerford Market, and palatial

hotels have been built where the gardens of Northumberland House once were. St.-Martin's-in-the-Fields is still in its wonted place, but with a change for the worse, in that the platform with its ascending steps has been curtailed during a recent alleged improvement in the roadway in St. Martin's Lane.

The National Gallery remains as of yore, except that it has recently been isolated by pulling down some adjoining structures to the northwest, as a precautionary measure against fire.

The Nelson Monument in Trafalgar Square, then newly arrived, is as it was in the days of Dickens' early life. But there is little suggestion in the hotel or its surroundings of its ever having been a "mouldy sort of an establishment in a close neighbourhood," and it is hard to believe that Copperfield's bedroom "smelt like a hackney-coach and was shut up like a family vault."

DICKENS' LITERARY LIFE

A BRIEF account is here given of Dickens' literary career, which presents chronologically a review of his productions as they appeared. The first of his literary efforts was the tragedy of "The Sultan of India," written in his precocious school-days at Chatham, when, if we except his Parliamentary journalistic work, nothing else was put forth until "The Dinner at Poplar Walk" was published in the *Monthly Magazine* (1833). The original "Sketches by Boz" — the first of which bore no signature — also followed in the *Monthly Magazine*. Other sketches under the same generic title also appeared in the *Evening Chronicle*, and yet others, under the title of "Scenes and Characters," were published in "Bell's Life in London" and the "Library of Fiction."

In 1836 a number of these fugitive pieces were collected into a volume, the copyright of which was sold to one Macrone for £100, who published them

under the first and best known title, " Sketches by
Boz." The familiar story of " Pickwick," its early
conception and its final publication, is well known.
Its first publication (in parts) dated from 1836-37.
About this time Dickens had another bad attack
of stage-fever, and wrote a farce, " The Strange
Gentleman," the libretto of an opera called " The
Village Coquettes," and a comedy, " Is She His
Wife?" more particularly perhaps for amateur rep-
resentation, in which he was very fond of taking
part. " Oliver Twist," a courageous attack on the
Poor Laws and Bumbledom, followed in 1838,
though it was not completed until after " Nicholas
Nickleby " began to appear in 1839.

At this time was started *Master Humphrey's
Clock,* a sort of miscellany in which it was intended
to publish a series of papers written chiefly by Dickens himself after the style of Addison's *Spectator*
of a former day. It was not at first successful, and
only upon the commencement therein of the " Old
Curiosity Shop " did it take on in any sense.

Master Humphrey's Clock ran down with the
completion of the novel, though this story, in company with " Barnaby Rudge," a tale of the riots of
'80, was not issued in book form until 1848 and
18.'9.

The authorship of " Pickwick " was unknown by

the great mass of the public until very nearly the completion of the work in serial parts. Much conjecture was raised, and a writer in *Bentley's Miscellany* published the following lines under the title of:

IMPROMPTU

" Who the Dickens ' Boz ' could be
Puzzled many a learned elf,
Till time revealed the mystery,
And ' Boz ' appeared as Dickens' self."

The other contributions made by Dickens to this periodical were afterward added to his published works under the title of " Master Humphrey's Clock."

Dickens' first tour to America followed the abandonment of the periodical in 1842. This event called forth the following verses by Tom Hood, entitled:

TO CHARLES DICKENS

On his Proposed Voyage to America, 1842.

" Pshaw ! away with leaf and berry
And the sober-sided cup !
Bring a Goblet and bright Sherry !
And a bumper fill me up. —
Tho' I had a pledge to shiver,
And the longest ever was, —
Ere his vessel leaves our river,
I will drink a health to ' Boz.'

" Here's success to all his antics,
Since it pleases him to roam,
And to paddle o'er Atlantics,
After such a sale *at home*
May he shun all rocks whatever,
And the shallow sand that lurks, —
And his passage be as clever
As the best among his works."

With what favour his visit was received in America is too well known to require detailed mention
here. His experiences and observations recounted
in " American Notes," first published in 1842 upon
his return to England, has told these vividly and
picturesquely, if not exactly consistently.

As a reader, Dickens stood as preëminently to the
fore as when posing as a writer. His phenomenal
success on the platform is given in detail in a volume written by George Dolby, who accompanied
him and managed his American tour. The mental
and physical strain was such that in fifteen years
of combined editorial, literary, and reading labours,
it left him attenuated and finally curtailed his bril-
liant work.

What the readings really did accomplish was to
increase and firmly assure the permanence of his
already wide-spread fame.

" Martin Chuzzlewit " had begun to appear in
shilling parts in 1843, and at that time was con-

sidered by the novelist to be by far the best work he had yet written. "Dombey and Son" followed, and afterward "David Copperfield," to which Dickens transferred his affections from "Chuzzlewit." This new "child of fancy," as he called it, was so largely autobiographical as to be accepted by many as being a recounting of his own early struggles as a poor boy in London, and his early literary labours. He himself said: "I seemed to be sending a part of myself into the shadowy world."

While "Chuzzlewit" was appearing in serial form, that masterpiece perhaps of all Dickens' shorter stories, "A Christmas Carol," — the first of the "Christmas Stories," — appeared.

This earned for its author the sobriquet, "The Apostle of Christmas."

Its immediate popularity and success was, perhaps, influenced by the following endorsement from Thackeray:

"It seems to me a national benefit, and to every man or woman who reads it a personal kindness."

Others under the same generic title followed: "The Chimes," 1844; "The Cricket on the Hearth," 1845; "The Battle of Life," 1846; and "The Haunted Man," 1848. In January, 1846, Dickens began his short connection with the *Daily News*.

Here his " Pictures from Italy " appeared, he having just returned from a journey thither.

"Dombey and Son," which Dickens had begun at Rosemont, Lausanne, took him from 1846 to 1848 to complete.

In 1850 the idea of *Household Words*, the periodical with which Dickens' fame is best remembered, took shape. His idea was for a low-priced periodical, to be partly original, and in part selected. " I want to suppose," he wrote, "a certain shadow which may go into any place by starlight, moonlight, sunlight, or candle-light, and be in all homes and all nooks and corners." The general outlines and plans were settled, but there appears to have been no end of difficulty in choosing a suitable name. " The Highway of Life," " The Holly Tree," " The Household Voice," " The Household Guest." and many others were thought of, and finally was hit upon " Household Words," the first number of which appeared on March 30, 1850, with the opening chapters of a serial by Mrs. Gaskell, whose work Dickens greatly admired. In number two appeared Dickens' own pathetic story, " The Child's Dream of a Star." In 1859, as originally conceived, *Household Words* was discontinued. from no want of success, but as an expediency brought about through disagreement among the various proprietors. Dickens bought the property in, and started afresh under the title of *All the Year Round*, among whose contributors were Edmund Yates, Percy Fitzgerald, Charles Lever, Wilkie Collins, Charles Reade, and Lord Lytton. This paper in turn came to its finish, and phœnix-like took shape again as *Household Words*, which in one form or another has endured to the present day, its present editor (1903) being Hall Caine, Jr., a son of the novelist.

Apart from the general circulation, the special Christmas numbers had an enormous sale. In these appeared other of the shorter pieces which have since become famous, — " Mugby Junction," " The Seven Poor Travellers," " The Haunted House," etc.

In the pages of *Household Words* " The Child's History of England," " The Uncommercial Traveller " (1861), and " Hard Times " (1854) first appeared; while *All the Year Round* first presented " A Tale of Two Cities " (1859) and " Great Expectations."

" Bleak House " was issued in parts in 1852. " Little Dorrit," originally intended to be called " Nobody's Fault," was published in 1857.

" Our Mutual Friend " dates from 1865 in book form. " Edwin Drood " was left unfinished at the author's death in 1870.

In 1868 "The Uncommercial Traveller" was elaborated for the first issue in *All the Year Round*, and subsequently again given to the world in revised book form.

Curiously enough, though most of Dickens' works were uncompleted before they began to appear serially, they have been universally considered to show absolutely no lack of continuity, or the least semblance of being in any way disjointed.

Dickens' second visit to America in 1867 was, like its predecessor, a stupendous success. A New York paper stated at this time that: "Of the millions here who treasure every word he has written, there are tens of thousands who would make a large sacrifice to see and hear a man who has made so many happy hours."

Dickens' fame had deservedly attracted a large circle of acquaintances around him, who, in truth, became firmly converted into fast friends.

His literary life and his daily labours had so identified him with the literary London of the day that all reference to literary events of that time must make due allowance of his movements.

The house at 48 Doughty Street still stands, and at the end of 1839 the novelist removed to the "handsome house with a considerable garden" in Devonshire Terrace, near Regent's Park, the subject

DICKENS' HOUSE IN DEVONSHIRE TERRACE.
From a drawing by Maclise.

NO. 48 DOUGHTY STREET, WHERE DICKENS LIVED.

of a sketch by Maclise which is here given. His
holidays during his early and busy years were spent
at Broadstairs, Twickenham, and Petersham on the
Thames, just above Richmond. Dickens was always
a great traveller, and his journeys often took him
far afield.

In 1841 he visited Landor at Bath, and in the
same year he made an excursion to Scotland and
was granted the freedom of the city of Edinburgh.
The first visit to America was undertaken in 1842;
his Italian travels in 1844; residence in Switzer-
land 1846; three months in Paris 1847; Switzer-
land and Italy revisited in 1853. Three summers
were spent at Boulogne in 1853, 1854, 1856; residence in Paris 1855-56; America revisited 1867-68.

Such in brief is a review of the physical activities
of the author. He did not go to Australia — as
he was variously importuned — but enough is given
to show that, in spite of his literary associations
with old London and its institutions, Charles Dickens was, for a fact, a very cosmopolitan observer.

As for Dickens' daily round of London life,
it is best represented by the period of the magazines,
Master Humphrey's Clock, Household Words, and
All the Year Round, particularly that of the former.
In those days he first met with the severe strain

which in after life proved, no doubt, to have short-
ened his days.

Considering his abilities and his early vogue,
Dickens made some astonishingly bad blunders in
connection with his agreements with publishers; of
these his biographer Forster tells in detail.

After the publication of "Martin Chuzzlewit,"
Dickens expressed dissatisfaction with his publishers, Messrs. Chapman and Hall, which resulted in
his making an agreement with Messrs. Bradbury
and Evans.

To conserve his intellectual resources, he resolved
to again visit Italy, to which country he repaired
after a farewell dinner given him at Greenwich,
where Turner, the artist, and many other notables
attended. He accordingly settled in a suburb of
Genoa, where he wrote "The Chimes," and came
back to London especially to read it to his friends.
Writing from Genoa to Forster in November, 1844,
he said:

". . . But the party for the night following?
I know you have consented to the party. Let me
see. Don't have any one this particular night for
dinner, but let it be a summons for the special purpose, at half-past six. Carlyle indispensable, and
I should like his wife of all things; *her* judgment
would be invaluable. You will ask Mac, and why

THE READING OF "THE CHIMES" AT FORSTER'S HOUSE IN LINCOLN'S INN FIELDS.

From a drawing by D. Maclise.

not his sister? Stanny and Jerrold I should particularly wish; Edwin Landseer, Blanchard . . . and when I meet you, oh! Heaven, what a week we will have!"

Forster further describes the occasion itself as being —

"Rather memorable . . . the germ of those readings to larger audiences by which, as much as by his books, the world knew him."

Among those present was Maclise, who, says Forster, "made a note of it" in pencil, which is reproduced herein. "It will tell the reader all he can wish to know, and he will thus see of whom the party consisted."

Of Dickens' entire literary career nothing was more successful than his famous public readings. From that night at Forster's house in Lincoln's Inn Fields (No. 58, still standing, 1903), afterward made use of as Mrs. Tulkinghorn's in "Bleak House," and later among other friends, at first in a purely informal and private manner and in a semi-public way for charitable objects, these diversions, so powerful and realistic were they, ultimately grew into an out-and-out recognized business enterprise.

The first series was inaugurated in 1858-59, and absolutely took the country by storm, meeting with the greatest personal affection and respect wherever he went. In Dublin there was almost a riot. People broke the pay-box, and freely offered £5 for a stall. In Belfast he had enormous audiences, being compelled, he said, to turn half the town away. The reading over, the people ran after him to look at him. "Do me the honour," said one, "to shake hands, Misther Dickens, and God bless you, sir; not ounly for the light you've been to me this night, but for the light you've been to mee house, sir (and God bless your face!), this many a year." Men cried undisguisedly.

During the second American tour, in 1867, the public went almost mad. In Boston his reception was beyond all expectations; and in New York the speculators assembled the night before the reading in long lines to wait the opening of the doors at nine the next morning for the issue of the tickets. They continued to come all night, and at five o'clock in the morning there were two lines of eight hundred each, whilst at eight there were five thousand. At nine o'clock, each of the two lines reached more than three-quarters of a mile in length, members of the families were relieving each other, waiters from neighbouring restaurants were serving breakfasts in the open December air, and excited applicants for tickets offering five or ten dollars for the mere permission to exchange places with other persons standing nearer the head of the line. Excitement and enthusiasm increased wherever he travelled, and it has been freely observed by all who knew him well that this excitement and strain finally culminated, after he had returned to England and undertaken there another series of readings, in an illness which hastened his death.

THE HIGHWAY OF LETTERS

*I*N Dickens' time, as in our own, and even
at as early a period as that of Drayton,
Fleet Street, as it has latterly been known,
has been the abode of letters and of literary labours.

The diarists, journalists, political and religious
writers of every party and creed have adopted it as
their own particular province. Grub Street no
longer exists, so that the simile of Doctor Johnson
does not still hold true.

The former Grub Street — "inhabited by writers of small histories, dictionaries, and temporary
poems" (*vide* Doctor Johnson's Dictionary) — has
become Milton Street through the mindful regard of some former sponsor, by reason of the
nearness of its location to the former Bunhill residence of the great epic poet. But modern Fleet
Street exists to-day as the street of journalists and
journalism, from the humble penny-a-liner and his
product to the more sedate and verbose political

paragrapher whose reputation extends throughout the world.

Nowhere else is there a long mile of such an atmosphere, redolent of printers' ink and the bustle attendant upon the production and distribution of the printed word. And nowhere else is the power of the press more potent.

Its historian has described it as "a line of street, with shops and houses on either side, between Temple Bar and Ludgate Hill, one of the largest thoroughfares in London, and one of the most famous."

Its name was derived from the ancient streamlet called the Fleet, more commonly "Fleet Ditch," near whose confluence with the Thames, at Ludgate Hill, was the notorious Fleet Prison, with its equally notorious "marriages."

This reeking abode of mismanagement was pulled down in 1844, when the "Marshalsea," "The Fleet," and the "Queen's Bench" (all three reminiscent of Dickens, likewise Newgate, not far away) were consolidated in a new structure erected elsewhere.

The unsavoury reputation of the old prison of the Fleet, its "chaplains," and its "marriages," are too well-known to readers of contemporary literature to be more than mentioned here.

The memory of the famous persons who were

at one time or another confined in this "noisome place with a pestilential atmosphere" are recalled by such names as Bishop Hooper, the martyr; Nash, the poet and satirist; Doctor Donne, Killigrew, the Countess of Dorset, Viscount Falkland, William Prynne, Richard Savage, and — of the greatest possible interest to Americans — William Penn, who lived "within the rules" in 1707.

The two churches lying contiguous to this thoroughfare, St. Dunstan's-in-the-West and St. Bride's, are mentioned elsewhere; also the outlying courts and alleys, such as Falcon, Mitre, and Salisbury Courts, Crane Court, Fetter Lane, Chancery Lane, Whitefriars, Bolt Court, Bell Yard, and Shoe Lane, the Middle and Inner Temples, and Sergeant's Inn.

The great fire of London of 1666 stopped at St. Dunstan's-in-the-West and at the easterly confines of the Temple opposite.

Michael Drayton, the poet, lived at "a baye-windowed house next the east end of St. Dunstan's Church," and Cowley was born "near unto the corner of Chancery Lane."

The "Horn Tavern," near which was Mrs. Salmon's celebrated waxwork exhibition (for which species of entertainment the street had been famous since Elizabeth's time), is now Anderton's

Hotel, still a famous house for "pressmen," the name by which the London newspaper writer is known.

A mere mention of the sanctity of letters which surrounded the Fleet Street of a former day is presumably the excuse for connecting it with the later development of literary affairs, which may be said, so far as its modern repute is concerned, to have reached its greatest and most popular height in Dickens' own time.

The chroniclers, the diarists, and the satirists had come and gone. Richardson — the father of the English novel — lay buried in St. Bride's, and the innovation of the great dailies had passed the stage of novelty. *The Gentleman's Magazine* and the Reviews had been established three-quarters of a century before. *The Times* had just begun to be printed by steam. Each newspaper bore an imprinted government stamp of a penny per copy, — a great source of revenue in that the public paid it, not the newspaper proprietor. (*The Times* then sold for five pence per copy.) The *Illustrated London News*, the pioneer of illustrated newspapers, had just come into existence, and *Punch*, under Blanchard and Jerrold, had just arrived at maturity, so to speak. Such, in a brief way, were the beginnings of the journalism of our day; and Dickens'

connection therewith, as Parliamentary reporter of
The True Sun and *The Morning Chronicle*, were
the beginnings of his days of assured and adequate
income, albeit that it came to him at a comparatively
early period of his life. The London journalist
of Dickens' day was different in degree only from
the present. *The True Sun*, for which Dickens
essayed his first reportorial work, and later *The
Morning Chronicle*, were both influential journals,
and circulated between them perhaps forty thousand
copies, each bearing a penny stamp impressed on
the margin, as was the law.

The newspapers of London, as well as of most
great cities, had a localized habitation, yclept
Newspaper Row or Printing-House Square, and
other similar appellations. In London the majority of them were, and are, printed east of Temple
Bar, in, or south of, Fleet Street, between Waterloo
and Blackfriars Bridges. To borrow Johnson's
phrase, this is the mart " whose staple is news."

The Times — " The Thunderer " of old — was
housed in a collection of buildings which surrounded
Printing-House Square, just east of Blackfriars
Bridge. In 1840 *The Times* had, or was understood
to have, three editors, fifteen reporters, with a more
or less uncertain and fluctuating number of corre-
spondents, news collectors, and occasional contrib-

utors. These by courtesy were commonly referred
to as the intellectual workers. For the rest, com-
positors, pressmen, mechanics, clerks, *et al.*, were of
a class distinct in themselves. The perfecting press
had just come into practical use, and though the
process must appear laboriously slow to-day when
only 2,500 *perfected* copies of a four-page paper
were turned out in an hour, *The Times* was in
its day at the head of the list as to organization,
equipment, and influence.

The other morning and evening papers, *The Post,
The Advertiser, The Globe, The Standard, The
Morning Chronicle,* and *The Sun,* all had similar
establishments though on a smaller scale.

But two exclusively literary papers were issued
in 1840 — *The Literary Gazette* and *The Athenæum,* the latter being to-day the almost universal
mentor and guide for the old-school lover of literature throughout the world. *The Spectator* was
the most vigorous of the weekly political and social
papers, now sadly degenerated, and *Bell's Life in
London,* which had printed some of Dickens' earlier
work, was the only nominal "sporting paper."
Church papers, trade papers, society papers, and
generally informative journals were born, issued for
a time, then died in those days as in the present.

Punch was, and is, the most thoroughly representative British humourous journal, and since its birth in the forties has been domiciled in Bouverie Street, just off the main thoroughfare of Fleet Street.

The literary production in this vast workshop in point of bulk alone is almost beyond comprehension. In 1869, a year before Dickens' death, there were published in London alone three hundred and seventy-two magazines and serials, seventy-two quarterlies, and two hundred and ninety-eight newspapers, etc.

As for the golden days of the "Highway of Letters," they were mostly in the glorious past, but, in a way, they have continued to this day. A brief review of some of the more important names and events connected with this famous street will, perhaps, not be out of place here.

Among the early printers and booksellers were Wynken de Worde, "at ye signe of ye Sonne;" Richard Pynson, the title-pages or colophons of whose works bore the inscription, "emprynted by me Richard Pynson at the temple barre of London (1493);" Rastell, "at the sign of the Star;" Richard Tottel, "within Temple-bar, at the signe of the Hande and Starre," which in Dickens' day had become the shop of a low bookseller by the name of Butterworth, who it was said still held the original leases. Others who printed and published in the vicinity were W. Copeland, "at the signe of the Rose Garland;" Bernard Lintot, "at the Cross Keys;" Edmund Curll, "at the Dial and Bible," and Lawton Gulliver, "at Homer's Head," against St. Dunstan's Church; and Jacob Robinson, on the west side of the gateway "leading down the Inner Temple Lane," an establishment which Dickens must have known as Groom's, the confectioner's. Here Pope and Warburton first met, and cultivated an acquaintanceship which afterward developed into as devoted a friendship as ever existed between man and man. The fruit of this was the publication (in 1739) of a pamphlet which bore the title, "A Vindication of Mr. Pope's 'Essay on Man,' by the Author of 'The Divine Legation of Moses,' printed for J. Robinson."

At Collins' shop, "at the Black Boy in Fleet Street," was published the first "Peerage," while other names equally famous were the publishers, T. White, H. Lowndes, and John Murray.

Another trade which was firmly established here was the bankers, "Child's," at Temple Bar, being the oldest existing banking-house in London to-day. Here Richard Blanchard and Francis Child, "at the Marygold in Fleet Street," — who were gold-smiths with "*running cashes*," — were first established in the reign of Charles II. "In the hands of Mr. Blanchard, goldsmith, next door to Temple Bar," Dryden deposited his £50 received for the discovery of the "bullies" by whom Lord Rochester had been barbarously assaulted in Covent Garden.

Another distinctive feature of Fleet Street was the taverns and coffee-houses. "The Devil," "The King's Head," at the corner of Chancery Lane, "The Bolt-in-Tun," "The Horn Tavern," "The Mitre," "The Cock," and "The Rainbow," with "Dick's," "Nando's," and "Peel's," at the corner of Fetter Lane, — its descendant still existing, — completes the list of the most famous of these houses of entertainment.

To go back to a still earlier time, to connect therewith perhaps the most famous name of English literature, bar Shakespeare, it is recorded that Chaucer "once beat a Franciscan friar in Fleet Street," and was fined two shillings for the privilege by the Honourable Society of the Inner Temple. As the chroniclers have it: "So Speght heard from Master Barkly, who had seen the entry in the records of the Inner Temple."

A rather gruesome anecdote is recounted by Hughson in his "Walks through London" (1817), concerning Flower-de-Luce Court (Fleur-de-Lis Court), just off Fetter Lane in Fleet Street.

This concerned the notorious Mrs. Brownrigg, who was executed in 1767 for the murder of Mary Clifford, her apprentice. " The grating from which the cries of the poor child issued " being still existent at the time when Hughson wrote and presumably for some time after. Canning, in imitation of Southey, recounts it thus in verse:

> " . . . Dost thou ask her crime?
> She whipp'd two female 'prentices to death,
> And hid them in the coal-hole. For this act
> Did Brownrigg swing. Harsh laws! But time shall come,
> When France shall reign and laws be all repeal'd."

Which gladsome (?) day has fortunately not yet come.

No résumé of the attractions of Fleet Street·can well be made without some mention of Whitefriars, that region comprehended between the boundaries of the Temple on one side, and where once was the Fleet Ditch on the other. Its present day association with letters mostly has to do with journalism, Carmelite Street, Whitefriars Street, and other lanes and alleys of the immediate neighbourhood being given over to the production of the great daily and weekly output of printed sheets. This ancient precinct formerly contained the old church of the White Friars, a community known in full as *Fratres Beatæ Mariæ de Mont Carmeli.*

Founded by Sir Richard Grey in 1241, the church was surrendered at the Reformation, and the Hall was made into the first Whitefriars Theatre, and the precinct newly named Alsatia, celebrated in modern literature by Scott in the "Fortunes of Nigel." "The George Tavern," mentioned in Shadwell's play, "The Squire of Alsatia," became later the printing shop of one Bowyer, and still more recently the printing establishment of Messrs. Bradbury and Evans, the publishers and proprietors of *Punch,* which building was still more recently removed for the present commodious structure occupied by this firm. In Dickens' time it was in part at least the old "George Tavern." It is singular perhaps that Dickens' connection with the famous "Round Table" of *Punch* was not more intimate than it was. It is not known that a single article of his was ever printed in its pages, though it is to be presumed he contributed several, and one at least is definitely acknowledged.

Ram Alley and Pye Corner were here in Alsatia, the former a passage between the Temple and Sergeant's Inn, which existed until recently.

Mitre Court is perhaps the most famous and revered of all the purlieus of Fleet Street. "The Mitre Tavern," or rather a reminiscence of it, much frequented by the London journalist of to-day and

of Dickens' time, still occupies the site of a former
structure which has long since disappeared, where
Johnson used to drink his port, and where he made
his famous remark to Ogilvie with regard to the
noble prospects of Scotland: "I believe, sir, you
have a great many; but, sir, let me tell you, I
believe, sir, you have a great many . . . but, sir,
let me tell you the noblest prospect which a Scotch-
man ever sees is the highroad that leads him to
England."

Of all the old array of taverns of Fleet Street,
"The Cock" most recently retained a semblance,
at least, of its former characteristics, which recalls
one of Tennyson's early poems, "A Monologue
of Will Waterproof," which has truly immortalized
this house of refreshment:

> "*Thou plump head-waiter at the Cock*
> *To which I must resort,*
> *How goes the time? Is't nine o'clock?*
> *Then fetch a pint of port.*"

Salisbury Court, or Salisbury Square as it has
now become, is another of those literary suburbs of
Fleet Street — if one may so call it — where modern literature was fostered and has prospered. It
occupies the courtyard of Salisbury or Dorset
House. Betterton, Cave, and Sandford, the actors,

lived here; Shadwell. Lady Davenant, the widow of the laureate; Dryden and Richardson also. Indeed Richardson wrote " Pamela " here, and Goldsmith was his " press corrector."

DICKENS' CONTEMPORARIES

*W*HEN Scott was at the height of his popularity and reputation, cultivated and imaginative prose was but another expression of the older poesy. But within twenty-five years of Scott's concluding fictions, Dickens and Thackeray, and still later, George Eliot and Kingsley, had come into the mart with an entirely new brand of wares, a development unknown to Scott, and of a tendency which was to popularize literature far more than the most sanguine hopes of even Scott's own ambition.

There was more warmth, geniality, and general good feeling expressed in the printed page, and the people — that vast public which must ever make or mar literary reputations, if they are to be financially successful ones, which, after all, is the standard by which most reputations are valued — were ready and willing to support what was popularly supposed to stand for the spread of culture.

Biographers and critics have been wont to attribute this wide love for literature to the influence of

Scott. Admirable enough this influence was, to be sure, and the fact is that since his time books have been more pleasingly frank, candid, and generous. But it was not until Dickens appeared, with his almost immediate and phenomenal success, that the real rage for the novel took form.

The first magazine, *The Gentleman's,* and the first review, *The Edinburgh,* were contemporary with Scott's productions, and grew up quite independently, of course, but their development was supposed, rightly or wrongly, to be coincident with the influences which were set in motion by the publication of Scott's novels. Certainly they were sent broadcast, and their influence was widespread, likewise Scott's devotees, but his books were "hard reading" for the masses nevertheless, and his most ardent champion could hardly claim for him a tithe of the popularity which came so suddenly to Charles Dickens.

"Pickwick Papers" (1837) appeared only six years later than Scott's last works, and but eight years before Thackeray's "Vanity Fair." It was, however, a thing apart from either, with the defects and merits of its author's own peculiar and energetic style.

Jealousies and bickerings there doubtless were, in those days, as ever, among literary folk, but though there may have been many who were envious, few were impolite or unjust enough not to recognize the new expression which had come among them. One can well infer this by recalling the fact that Thackeray himself, at a Royal Academy banquet, had said that he was fearful of what " Pickwick's " reputation might have been had he succeeded in getting the commission, afterward given to Seymour, to illustrate the articles.

There appears to have been, at one time, some misunderstanding between Dickens and his publishers as to who really was responsible for the birth of " Pickwick," one claim having been made that Dickens was only commissioned to write up Seymour's drawings. This Dickens disclaimed emphatically in the preface written to a later edition, citing the fact that Seymour only contributed the few drawings to the first serial part, unfortunately dying before any others were even put in hand.

There is apparently some discrepancy between the varying accounts of this incident, but Dickens probably had the right of it, though the idea of some sort of a " Nimrod Club," which afterward took Dickens' form in the " Pickwickians," was thought of between his publishers and Seymour. In fact, among others, besides Dickens, who were consid-

ered as being able to do the text, were Theodore
Hook, Leigh Hunt, and Tom Hood.

As originally planned, it was undoubtedly a piece
of what is contemptuously known as hack work.
What it afterward became, under Dickens' master-
ful power, all the parties concerned, and the world
in general, know full well.

The statement that Dickens is "out of date,"
"not read now," or is "too verbose," is by the
mark when his work is compared with that of his
contemporaries. In a comparative manner he is
probably very much read, and very well read, too,
for that matter. Far more so, doubtless, than most
of his contemporaries; certainly before George
Eliot, Wilkie Collins, Bulwer, or even Carlyle or
Thackeray.

The very best evidence of this, if it is needed,
is to recall to what great extent familiarity with
the works of Dickens has crept into the daily life
of "the people," who more than ever form the great
majority of readers.

True, times and tastes have changed from even
a quarter of a century ago. Fashions come and go
with literature, novels in particular, as with all else,
and the works of Dickens, as a steady fare, would
probably pall on the most enthusiastic of his admirers. On the other hand, he would be a dull per-

son indeed who could see no humour in "Pickwick," whatever his age, creed, or condition. Admirers of the great novelist have been well looked after in respect to editions of his works. New ones follow each other nowadays in an extraordinarily rapid succession, and no series of classics makes its appearance without at least three or four of Dickens' works finding places in its list. In England alone there have been twenty-four complete copyright editions, from "the cheap edition," first put upon the market in 1847, to the dainty and charming India paper edition printed at the Oxford University Press in 1901.

"In the Athenæum Club," says Mr. Percy Fitzgerald, "where many a pleasant tradition is preserved, we may see at a window a table facing the United Service Club at which Dickens was fond of having his lunch. . . . In the hall by the coats (after their Garrick quarrel), Dickens and Thackeray met, shortly before the latter's death. A moment's hesitation, and Thackeray put out his hand . . . and they were reconciled."

It has been said, and justly, that Thackeray — Dickens' contemporary, not rival — had little of the topographical instinct which led to no small degree of Dickens' fame. It has, too, been further claimed that Thackeray was in debt to Dickens for having borrowed such expressions as " *the opposite side of Goswell Street was over the way.*" And such suggestions as the " Two jackals of Lord Steyne and Mess. Wegg and Wenham, reminiscent of Pike and Pluck, and Sedley's native servant, who was supposed to have descended from Bagstock's menial." Much more of the same sort might be recounted, all of which, if it is true, is perhaps no sin, but rather a compliment.

The relics and remains of Dickens exist to a remarkable degree of numbers. As is well known, the omnific American collector is yearly, nay daily, acquiring many of those treasures of literature and art which the old world has treasured for generations; to the gratification of himself and the pride of his country, though, be it said, to the disconcern of the Briton.

The American, according to his English cousin, it seems, has a pronounced taste for acquiring the rarest of Dickens' books, and the choicest of Dickens' holographs, and his most personal relics.

The committee of the " Dickens Fellowship," a newly founded institution to perpetuate the novelist's name and fame, recently sought to bring together in an exhibition held in Memorial Hall, London, as many of those souvenirs as possible; and a very attractive and interesting show it proved to be.

The catalogue of this exhibition, however, had tacked on to it this significant note: " The Committee's quest for literary memorabilia of the immortal ' Boz ' indicates the distressing fact that many of the rarest items are lost to us for ever."

All of which goes again to show that the great interest of Americans in the subject is, in a way, the excuse for being of this monograph on London during the life and times of Dickens.

Various exhibitions of Dickens' manuscripts have been publicly held in London from time to time, at The Exhibition of the Works of the English Humourists in 1889, at the Victorian Exhibition of 1897, and the British Museum has generally on show, in the " King's Library," a manuscript or two of the novels; there are many more always to be seen in the " Dyce and Forster Collection " at South Kensington. Never, before the exhibition held in 1902 by the " Dickens Fellowship," has there been one absolutely restricted to Dickens.

It is, of course, impossible to enumerate the various items, and it would not be meet that the attempt should be made here. It will be enough to say that among the many interesting numbers was the first portion of an unpublished travesty on "Othello," written in 1833, before the first published "Boz" sketch, and a hitherto unknown (to experts) page of "Pickwick," this one fragment being valued, says the catalogue, at £150 sterling. First editions, portraits, oil paintings, miniatures, and what not, and autographs were here in great numbers, presentation copies of Dickens' books, given to his friends, and autographs and portraits of his contemporaries, as well as the original sketches of illustrations to the various works by Seymour, "Phiz," Cruikshank, Stone, Leech, Barnard, and Pailthorpe, not forgetting a reference to the excellent work of our own Darley, and latterly Charles Dana Gibson.

Among the most interesting items of contemporary interest in this exhibition, which may be classed as unique, were presentation copies of the novels made to friends and acquaintances by Dickens himself.

Among them were "David Copperfield," a presentation copy to the Hon. Mrs. Percy Fitzgerald; "Oliver Twist," with the following inscription on the title-page, "From George Cruikshank to H. W. Brunton, March 19, 1872;" "A Child's History of England," with an autograph letter to Marcus Stone, R. A.; "A Tale of Two Cities," presented

to Mrs. Macready, with autograph; " The Chimes "
(Christmas Book, 1845), containing a unique impression of Leech's illustration thereto.

Other interesting and valuable *ana* were the
Visitors' Book of " Watts' Charity," at Rochester,
containing the signatures of " C. D." and Mark
Lemon; the quill pen belonging to Charles Dickens,
and used by him just previous to his death; a
paper-knife formerly belonging to " C. D.," and the
writing-desk used by " C. D." on his last American
tour; silver wassail-bowl and stand presented to
" C. D." by members of the Philosophical Institution of Edinburgh in 1858; walking-stick formerly
belonging to " C. D.; " a screen belonging to Moses
Pickwick, of Bath — the veritable Moses Pickwick
of Chap. XXXV. of " Pickwick Papers; " the oak
balustrade from the old " White Hart " (pulled
down in 1889); pewter tankards from various of
the Pickwickian Inns; the entrance door of Newgate Prison, of which mention is made in " Barnaby
Rudge," Chap. LXIV.; warrant officer's staff,
formerly in use in the Marshalsea Prison; original
sign of " The Little Wooden Midshipman "
(" Dombey and Son "), formerly over the doorway
of Messrs. Norie and Wilson, the nautical publishers in the Minories. This varied collection, of
which the above is only a mere selection, together

with such minor *personalia* as had been preserved
by friends and members of the family, formed a
highly interesting collection of Dickens' reliques,
and one whose like will hardly be got together again.

Innumerable portraits, photographs, lithographs,
and drawings of the novelist were included, as well
as of his friends and contemporaries.

Letters and documents referring to Dickens' relations with Shirley Brooks, Richard Bentley, Hablôt K. Browne, Frederic Chapman, J. P. Harley,
Mark Lemon, Samuel Rogers, Newby, John Forster, David Maclise, and many others, mostly unpublished, were shown, and should form a valuable
fund of material for a biographer, should he be
inclined to add to Dickens' literature of the day,
and could he but have access to and the privilege of
reprinting them.

A word on the beginnings of what is commonly
called serial literature is pertinent to the subject.
The first publication with which Dickens' identity
was solely connected was the issue of " Pickwick "
in monthly parts in 1836-37.

A literary critic, writing in 1849, had this to say
on the matter in general, with a further reference to
the appearance of " David Copperfield," whose author was the chief and founder of the serial novel:

" The small library which issues from the press on

the first of every month is a new and increasing
fashion in literature, which carves out works into
slices and serves them up in fresh portions twelve
times in the year. Prose and poetry, original and selected, translations and republications, of every class
and character, are included. The mere enumeration
of titles would require a vast space, and any attempt
to analyze the contents, or to estimate the influence
which the class exerts upon the literary taste of the
day would expand into a volume of itself. As an
event of importance must be mentioned the appearance of the first number of a new story, 'David
Copperfield,' by Charles Dickens. His rival humourist, Mr. Thackeray, has finished one and begun
another of his domestic histories within the twelve-
month, his new story, 'Pendennis,' having journeyed seven-twentieths of the way to completion.
Mr. Lever rides double with 'Roland Cashel' and
'Con Cregan,' making their punctual appearance
upon the appointed days. Of another order is Mr.
Jerrold's 'Man Made of Money.' Incidents are
of little consequence to this author, except by way
of pegs to hang reflections and conclusions upon.

"Passing over the long list of magazines and reviews as belonging to another class of publication,
there is a numerous series of reprints, new editions,
etc., issued in monthly parts, and generally in a

cheap and compendious form. Shakespeare and Byron among the poets, Bulwer, Dickens, and James among the novelists, appear pretty regularly, — the poets being enriched with notes and illustrations. Other writers and miscellaneous novels find republication in the ' Parlour Library of Fiction,' with so rigid an application of economy that for two shillings we may purchase a guinea and a half's worth of the most popular romances at the original price of publication. Besides the works of imagination, and above them in value, stand Knight's series of ' Monthly Volumes.' Murray's ' Home and Colonial Library,' and the ' Scientific ' and ' Literary Libraries ' of Mr. Bohn. The contents of these collections are very diversified; many volumes are altogether original, and others are new translations of foreign works, or modernized versions of antiquarian authors. A large mass of the most valuable works contained in our literature may be found in Mr. Bohn's ' Library.' The class of publications introduced in them all partakes but little of the serial character. It is only the form of their appearance which gives them a place among the periodicals."

In the light of more recent events and tendencies, this appears to have been the first serious attempt to popularize and broaden the sale of literature to any considerable extent, and it may be justly inferred that the cheap "Libraries," "Series," and "Reprints" of the present day are but an outgrowth therefrom.

As for Dickens' own share in this development, it is only necessary to recall the demand which has for many years existed for the original issues of such of the novels as appeared in parts. The earliest issues were: "The Pickwick Papers," in 20 parts, 1836-37, which contained the two suppressed Buss plates; "Nicholas Nickleby," in 20 parts, 1838-39; "Master Humphrey's Clock," in 88 weekly numbers, 1840-41; "Master Humphrey's Clock," in 20 monthly parts, 1840-41; "Martin Chuzzlewit," in 20 parts, 1843-44; "Oliver Twist," in 10 octavo parts, 1846.

At the time when "Oliver Twist" had scarce begun, Dickens was already surrounded by a large circle of literary and artistic friends and acquaintances. His head might well have been turned by his financial success, many another might have been so affected. His income at this time (1837-38) was supposed to have increased from £400 to £2,000 per annum, surely an independent position, were it an assured one for any litterateur of even the first rank, of Dickens' day or of any other.

In November of 1837 "Pickwick" was finished, and the event celebrated by a dinner "at the Prince of Wales" in Leicester Place, off Leicester Square. To this function Dickens had invited Talfourd, Forster, Macready, Harrison Ainsworth, Jerdan, Edward Chapman, and William Hall.

Dickens' letter to Macready was in part as follows:

"It is to celebrate (that is too great a word, but I can think of no better) the conclusion of my 'Pickwick' labours; and so I intend, before you take that roll upon the grass you spoke of, to beg your acceptance of one of the first complete copies of the work. I shall be much delighted if you would join us."

Of "Nicholas Nickleby," written in 1838-39, Sydney Smith, one of its many detractors, finally succumbed and admitted: "'Nickleby' is very good — I held out against Dickens as long as I could, but he has conquered me."

Shortly after the "Pickwick" dinner, and after the death of his wife's sister Mary, who lived with them, Dickens, his wife, and "Phiz," — Hablôt K. Browne, — the illustrator of "Pickwick," journeyed together abroad for a brief time. On his return, Dickens first made acquaintance with the seaside village of Broadstairs, where his memory still lives, preserved by an ungainly structure yclept "Bleak House."

CHARLES DICKENS, HIS WIFE, AND SISTER
GEORGINA.

From a pencil drawing by D. Maclise.

.

It may be permissible here to make further mention of Broadstairs. The town itself formed the subject of a paper which he wrote for *Household Words* in 1851, while as to the structure known as " Bleak House," it formed, as beforesaid, his residence for a short time in 1843.

Writing to an American friend, Professor Felton, at that time, he said:

" In a bay-window in a ' one pair ' sits, from nine o'clock to one, a gentleman with rather long hair and no neckcloth, who writes and grins as if he thought he were very funny indeed. His name is Boz. . . . He is brown as a berry, and they *do* say is a small fortune to the innkeeper who sells beer and cold punch. . . ."

Altogether a unique and impressive pen-portrait, and being from the hand of one who knew his sitter, should be considered a truthful one.

In 1843 Maclise made that remarkable and winsome pencil sketch of Dickens, his wife, and his sister Georgina, one of those fleeting impressions which, for depicting character and sentiment, is worth square yards of conventional portraiture, and which is reproduced here out of sheer admiration for its beauty and power as a record *intime*. It has been rather coarsely referred to in the past as Maclise's sketch of " Dickens and his pair of petticoats," but we let that pass by virtue of its own sweeping condemnation, — of its being anything more than a charming and intimate record of a fleeting period in the novelist's life, too soon to go — never to return.

Dickens' connection with the *Daily News* was but of brief duration; true, his partisans have tried to prove that it was under his leadership that it was launched upon its career. This is true in a measure, — he was its first editor, — but his tenure of office only lasted "*three short weeks.*"

He was succeeded in the editorial chair by his biographer, Forster.

The first number came out on January 21, 1846, — a copy in the recent "Dickens Fellowship Exhibition" (London, 1903) bore the following inscription in Mrs. Dickens' autograph: "Brought home by Charles at two o'clock in the morning. — Catherine Dickens. January 21." Thus it is that each issue of a great newspaper is born, or made, though the use of the midnight oil which was burned on this occasion was no novelty to Charles Dickens himself. The issue in question contained the first of a series of "Travelling Sketches — Written on the Road," which were afterward published in book form as "Pictures from Italy."

A unique circumstance of contemporary interest

to Americans occurred during Dickens' second
visit to America (1868) in "The Great International Walking Match." A London bookseller at
the present time (1903) has in his possession the
original agreement between George Dolby (British
subject), *alias* "The Man of Ross," and James
Ripley Osgood, *alias* "The Boston Bantam,"
wherein Charles Dickens, described as "The Gad's
Hill Gasper," is made umpire.

One of the most famous and interesting portraits
of Dickens was that made in pencil by Sir John
Millais, A. R. A., in 1870. This was the last pre-
sentment of the novelist, in fact, a posthumous
portrait, and its reproduction was for a long time
not permitted. The original hangs in the parlour
of "The Leather Bottle," at Cobham, given to the
present proprietor by the Rev. A. H. Berger, M. A.,
Vicar of Cobham. Among other famous portraits
of Dickens were those by Ary Scheffer, 1856; a
miniature on ivory by Mrs. Barrow, 1830; a pencil
study by "Phiz," 1837; a chalk drawing by Samuel
Lawrence, 1838; "The Captain Boabdil" portrait
by Leslie, 1846; an oil portrait by W. P. Frith,
R. A., 1859; a pastel portrait by J. G. Gersterhauer,
1861; and a chalk drawing by E. G. Lewis, 1869.
This list forms a chronology of the more important
items of Dickens portraiture from the earliest to

that taken after his death, subsequent to which was made a plaster cast, from which Thomas Woolner, R. A., modelled the bust portrait.

The " Boz Club," founded in 1899 by Mr. Percy Fitzgerald, one of Dickens' " bright young men " in association with him in the conduct of *Household Words* was originally composed of members of the Athenæum Club, of whom the following knew Dickens personally, Lord James of Hereford, Mr. Marcus Stone, R. A., and Mr. Luke Fildes, R. A., who, with others, foregathered for the purpose of dining together and keeping green the memory of the novelist.

Its membership has since been extended to embrace the following gentlemen, who also had the pleasure and gratification of acquaintanceship with Dickens: the Marquis of Dufferin and Ava (since died), Lord Brompton, Hamilton Aide, Alfred Austin, Sir Squire Bancroft, Arthur à Beckett, Francesco Berger, Henry Fielding Dickens, K. C., Edward Dicy, C. B., W. P. Frith, R. A., William Farrow, Otto Goldschmidt, John Hollingshead, the Very Reverend Dean Hole, Sir Henry Irving, Frederick A. Inderwick, K. C., Sir Herbert Jerningham, K. C., M. G., Charles Kent, Fred'k G. Kitton, Moy Thomas, Right Honourable Sir Arthur Otway, Bart., Joseph C. Parkinson, George Storey, A. R. A.,

J. Ashby Sterry, and Right Honourable Sir H.
Drummond Wolfe.

Perhaps the most whole-souled endorsement of
the esteem with which Dickens was held among
his friends and contemporaries was contributed to
the special Dickens' memorial number of *Household Words* by Francesco Berger, who composed
the incidental music which accompanied Wilkie
Collins' play, " The Frozen Deep," in which Dickens himself appeared in 1857:

" I saw a great deal of Charles Dickens personally
for many years. He was always most genial and
most hearty, a man whose friendship was of the
warmest possible character, and who put his whole
soul into every pursuit. He was most generous,
and his household was conducted on a very liberal
scale.

" I consider that, if not the first, he was among
the first, who went out of the highways into the
byways to discover virtue and merit of every kind
among the lower classes, and found romance in
the lowest ranks of life.

" I regard Dickens as the greatest social reformer
in England I have ever known outside politics.
His works have tended to revolutionize for the
better our law courts, our prisons, our hospitals,

our schools, our workhouses, our government offices, etc.

"He was a fearless exposer of cant in every direction, — religious, social, and political."

Such was the broad-gauge estimate of one who knew Dickens well. It may unquestionably be accepted as his greatest eulogy.

None of Dickens' contemporaries are more remembered and revered than the illustrators of his stories. Admitting all that can possibly be said of the types which we have come to recognize as being "Dickenesque," he would be rash who would affirm that none of their success was due to their pictorial delineation.

Dickens himself has said that he would have preferred that his stories were not illustrated, but, on the other hand, he had more than usual concern with regard thereto when the characters were taking form under the pencils of Seymour, Cruikshank, or "Phiz," or even the later Barnard, than whom, since Dickens' death, has there ever been a more sympathetic illustrator?

The greatest of these was undoubtedly George Cruikshank, whose drawings for "Oliver Twist," the last that he did for Dickens' writings, were perhaps more in keeping with the spirit of Dickens' text than was the work of any of the others, not excepting the immortal character of Pickwick, which conception is accredited to Seymour, who unfortunately died before he had completed the quartette of drawings for the second number of the serial.

In this same connection it is recalled that the idea of recounting the adventures of a " club of Cockney sportsmen " was conceived by the senior partner of the firm of Chapman and Hall, and that Dickens was only thought of at first as being the possible author, in connection, among others, with Leigh Hunt and Theodore Hook.

On the death of Seymour, one R. W. Buss, a draughtsman on wood, was commissioned to continue the " Pickwick " illustrations, and he actually made two etchings, which, in the later issues, were suppressed. " Crowquill," Leech, and Thackeray all hoped to fill the vacancy, but the fortunate applicant was Hablôt K. Browne, known in connection with his work for the Dickens stories as " Phiz." This *nom de plume* was supposed to have been adopted in order to harmonize with " Boz."

" Phiz " in time became known as the artist-in-chief, and he it was who made the majority of illustrations for the tales, either as etchings or wood-blocks. His familiar signature identifies his work to all who are acquainted with Dickens.

George Cattermole supplied the illustrations to " The Old Curiosity Shop " and " Barnaby Rudge." Of these Dickens has said " that it was the very first time that any of the designs for which he had written had touched him." Marcus Stone, R. A., provided the pictures for " Our Mutual Friend."

John Leech, of *Punch* fame, in one of his illustrations to " The Battle of Life," one of the shorter pieces, made the mistake of introducing a wrong character into one of the drawings, and a still more pronounced error was in the Captain Cuttle plates, where the iron hook appears first on the left and then on the right arm of the subject.

Leech illustrated the " Christmas Carol " complete, including the coloured plates, and shared in contributing to the other Yule-tide stories.

Of the leading artists who contributed the illustrations to Dickens' writings during his lifetime, it is notable that three were " Royal Academicians," — Stanfield, Maclise, and Landseer, — one an " Associate of the Royal Academy," and, besides those already mentioned, there were in addition Richard (Dicky) Doyle, John Leech, and (now Sir) John Tenniel, Luke Fildes, and Sir Edwin Landseer, who did one drawing only, that for " Boxer," the carrier-dog, in " The Cricket on the Hearth." Onwyn, Crowquill, Sibson, Kenney Meadows, and F.

W. Pailthorpe complete the list of those artists best known as contemporary with Dickens.

In creating the characters of his novels, as is well known, Dickens often drew upon his friends and acquaintances as models, and seldom did these effigies give offence. On one occasion the reverse was the case, as in "Bleak House," which was issued in 1857. Boythorne, who was drawn from his friend Landor, and Skimpole, from Leigh Hunt, were presumably so pertinent caricatures of the originals that they were subsequently modified in consequence.

Another incident of more than unusual importance, though not strictly dealing with any of Dickens' contemporaries, is a significant incident relating to the living worth of his work. It is related that when Bismarck and Jules Favre met under the walls of Paris, the former waiting to open fire upon the city, the latter was seen to be busily engrossed, quite oblivious of the situation, devouring "Little Dorrit." The story may be taken for what it appears to be worth; it is doubtful if it could be authenticated, but it serves to indicate the widespread and absorbing interest of the novels, and serves again to indicate that the power of the novel in general is one that will relax the faculties and

provide the stimulus which an active brain ofte:
fails to find otherwise.

Dickens had dedicated to Carlyle "Hard Times,"
which appeared as early as 1854, and paid a sti
further tribute to the Scotch genius when, in 1859
he had begun "A Tale of Two Cities."

In it he hoped to add something to the popula
and picturesque means of understanding the terribl
time of the French Revolution; "though no one,"
he said, "could hope to add anything to the philos
ophy of Carlyle's wonderful book." To-day it is
one of the most popular and most read of all his
works.

Dickens died on the 9th of June, 1870, leaving
"Edwin Drood" unfinished. What he had writter
of it appeared in the usual green paper parts and
afterward in volume form. In October, 1871, a
continuation entitled "John Jasper's Secret" began
to appear, and occupied eight monthly parts, produced uniformly with "Drood;" and recently a
gentleman in Holland sent the publishers — Messrs.
Chapman and Hall — a completion written by himself. There were other attempts of this nature, but
Dickens' book must always remain as he left it.

That a reference to the "Poets' Corner" in Westminster Abbey might properly be included in a sec-

DICKENS' GRAVE IN WESTMINSTER ABBEY.

.

tion of this book devoted to the contemporaries of Charles Dickens, no one perhaps will deny.

It seems fitting, at least, that it should be mentioned here rather than elsewhere, in that the work

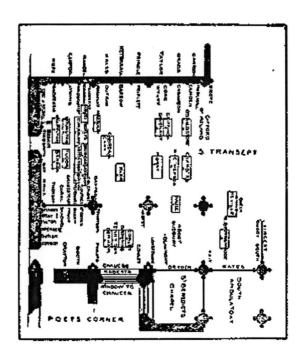

does not pretend to be a categorical guide to even the more important sights of London, but merely that it makes mention of those sights and scenes, places and peoples, more or less intimately associated with the great novelist.

Charles Dickens was buried in Westminster Abbey on the 14th June, 1870, since which time

various other graves have been made, Browning
and Tennyson notably, and monuments and me-
morials put into place of Longfellow and Ruskin.

The Poets' Corner occupies about half of the
south transept of Westminster Abbey. This famous place for the busts and monuments of eminent
men includes those of Chaucer, Spencer, Shakespeare, Drayton, Ben Jonson, Milton, Butler, Davenant, Cowley, Dryden, Prior, Rowe, Gay, Addison,
Thomson, Goldsmith, Gray, Mason, Sheridan,
Southey, Campbell, etc. Lord Macaulay and Lord
Palmerston were buried here in 1860 and 1865.
Thackeray is not buried here, but at Kensal Green,
though his bust is placed next to the statue of Joseph
Addison. Dickens' grave is situated at the foot of
the coffin of Handel, and at the head of the coffin of
R. B. Sheridan. More recently, Doctor Livingstone,
the celebrated African traveller, was buried here.
Near to England's great humourist, toward his feet,
lie Doctor Johnson and Garrick, while near them
lies Thomas Campbell. Shakespeare's monument is
not far from the foot of the grave. Goldsmith's
is on the left.

THE LOCALE OF THE NOVELS

*I*F one may make legitimate use of the term,
"the topography of Dickens," — which an
English writer coined many years since,
— it may well be indiscriminately applied to Dickens' own life and that of the characters of his
stories as well.

The subject has ever been a favourite one which
has cropped up from time to time in the "bitty"
literature of the last quarter of a century.

To treat it exhaustively would be impossible; the
changes and progress of the times will not permit
of this. Nothing would be final, and new shadows
would constantly be thrown upon the screen.

Dickens' observation, as is well known, was
most keen, but he mostly saw only those things
which, in some degree, actually existed, — towns.
villages, streets, localities, and public and private
houses. Not an unusual method of procedure for
many an author of repute, but few have had the
finesse to lay on local colour to the extent used by

Dickens, without tending toward mere description. This no one has ever had the temerity to lay to Dickens' door.

Mention can be made herein of but a few of the localities, many of which had existed to very near the present day.

To enumerate or to even attempt to trace them all would be practically impossible, but enough has been authenticated to indicate a more substantial reality than is found in the work of any other modern English author.

If one is so minded, he can start out from the very hotel, — "The Golden Cross" at Charing Cross, — from which Pickwick and Jingle started on their coach ride to Rochester, and where Copperfield and Steerforth also stayed. The "dark arches of the Adelphi," the Temple, and Fountain Court, remain much as of yore.

Fleet Street was well known to Dickens, and has changed but little, and Lincoln's Inn Fields, Bloomsbury, and many other localities have in reality changed not at all in their relation to their environment. In matters of detail they have, of course, in many instances undergone a certain remoulding, which is no greater perhaps than the usual liberties taken by the average author.

Dickens, in the main, changed the surroundings

YORK WATER GATE.

ENTRANCE TO ADELPHI ARCHES.

of his scenes — which he may have given another
name — but little.

"Copperfield" is redolent of his own early associations and experiences in London. The neighbourhood of Charing Cross will be first called to
mind. Hungerford Market and Hungerford Bridge
(as the present Charing Cross Railway Bridge is
often called by the old resident), and the "Adelphi,"
with its gruesome arches beneath, all give more than
a suggestion of the sights and scenes which met
Dickens' own eye when his personality was closely
associated therewith.

Hence, regardless of whether it is biography or
pure fiction, there are to-day substantial reminders
throughout London, not only of his life but of the
very scenes associated with the characters of his
novels. More particularly in the early novels,
"Pickwick," "Nickleby," and "Copperfield," are
their topographical features to be most readily recognized, because, in the first place, they are, presumably, the more familiar; and secondly, because
they are more vividly recalled.

It is a fact, however, that in Dickens' sketches and
tales, and in many of his minor works, as, for instance, in the pages of "Master Humphrey's Clock,"
there are passages especially concerning persons and
places in London, which to-day have, as then, a

stern reality, referring to such familiar spots as the
site of the Marshalsea Prison, or " The Old White
Horse," or Peggotty's Yarmouth home.

Reality or imagination, — it's all the same, —
Dickens drew in his pictures, after a veritable fashion, this too, in spite of the precedent of a former
generation of authors, who had for ages, one may
say centuries, tilled the field over and over. But
it was not until Dickens " arrived " that the reading
world in general, and wherever found, acquired that
nodding acquaintance with London which has since
so redounded to this author's reputation. No such
acquaintance was previously to be had with the contemporary London life of the middle and lower
classes, if one may be pardoned for expressing it
thus confidently.

The marvel is that some ardent spirit has not
before now compiled an out-and-out Dickens guide-
book. One writer, at least, is recalled who is com-
petent to do it, and he, be it said, is an American,
Doctor Benjamin S. Martin, who many years ago
contributed to an American monthly publication a
series of illuminating articles on what might with
propriety be called the local colour of Dickens.
These were the forerunners and foster-parents of
most of the " scrappy " articles of a similar purport

which appear intermittently in the English and American periodical press.

The references and descriptions of certain of the localities connected with the novels which follow are given without attempt at classification or chronological arrangement. No other plan appears possible, where only a selection can be given. As before said, the limitations of the bulk of this book preclude a more extensive résumé.

The following references will be found to be fully classified in the index which accompanies the book, and will perhaps prove suggestive, at least, of further research on the part of the individual reader.

Further west, beyond Westminster and the Parliament Houses, is Milbank, where is Church Street, running from the river to St. John's Church, Westminster, that atrociously ill-mannered church of Queen Anne's day, built it is said on the lines of a footstool overturned in one of that lady's fits of petulant wrath. Down Church Street ran Martha, followed by Copperfield and Peggotty, bent on suicide.

Not the slum it was when described by Dickens, it is to-day a sufficiently " mean street " to be suggestive.

Here too, was Jenny Wren's house, on the left going toward the church in Smith Square.

Vauxhall Bridge, also reminiscent of Dickens, is near by, though the structure which formerly graced the site has given way to a temporary ungainly thing, which is neither beautiful to look upon nor suitable to its purpose.

In the neighbourhood of Charing Cross, on Craven Street, at No. 8, is still the door-knocker which so looked, to Marley, like a human face.

In Chandos Street, till within the last eight or ten years, were two old-time shops, to which Warren's Blacking Factory removed before the boy Dickens left their employ.

In Chandos Street, too, were the "pudding-shop" and "à la mode beef-shop," of which Dickens made such emphatic mention to his biographer, Forster.

At the corner of Parliament Street and Whitehall, in Westminster, was, until the beginning of the twentieth century, the "Old Red Lion" public house, which calls to mind the episode of "the very best stunning ale" in "Copperfield," but which is reputedly attributed as actually happening to Dickens himself.

Chancery Lane is largely identified with the story of "Bleak House." The garden of Lincoln's Inn

RESIDENCE OF JOHN FORSTER, LINCOLN'S INN FIELDS.

was fondly referred to by little Miss Flite as " her garden." Law offices, stationers' shops, and eating-houses abound in the purlieus of Chancery Lane, which, though having undergone considerable change in the last quarter-century, has still, in addition to the majesty which is supposed to surround the law, something of those " disowned relations of the law and hangers-on " of which Dickens wrote.

In this immediate neighbourhood — in Lincoln's Inn Fields — was Mrs. Tulkinghorn's house, of which an illustration is here given, and which is still standing (1903). This house, which is readily found, — it is still No. 58, — is now given over to lawyers' offices, though formerly it was the residence of Dickens' biographer, Forster, where Dickens gave what was practically the first of his semi-public readings, on the occasion when he came from Italy especially to read the " Christmas story," " The Chimes," to a few favoured friends.

Hard by, just off the southwestern corner of the square, is the apocryphal " Old Curiosity Shop," a notable literary shrine, as is mentioned elsewhere, but not the original of the novel which bears the same name, as Dickens himself has said.

The " Clare Market," an unsavoury locality which had somewhat to do with " Pickwick," was near by, but has practically disappeared from view in a virtuous clearing-up process which has recently been undertaken.

In Portugal Street, leading into Lincoln's Inn Fields, was Mr. Solomon's headquarters; while further east, toward the city, we find the "George and Vulture," mentioned in "Pickwick," existing to-day as "a very good old-fashioned and comfortable house." Its present nomenclature is "Thomas' Chop-House," and he who would partake of the "real thing" in good old English fare, served on pewter plates, with the brightest of steel knives and forks, could hardly fare better than in this ancient house in St. Michael's Alley.

By one of those popular and ofttimes sentimental conclusions, "poor Jo's crossing" has been located as being on Holborn, near where Chancery Lane comes into that thoroughfare.

This may like enough be so, but as all crossings are much alike, and all sweepers of that impoverished class which we recognize in the description of "Jo" (now luckily disappearing), it would seem a somewhat doubtful accomplishment in attempting to place such a spot definitely.

Mrs. Jellyby lived in Thavie's Inn, — "Only 'round the corner" from Chancery Lane, said Guppy, — one of the seven inns allied with the

four great Inns of Court, all of which had a particular sentiment for Dickens, both in his writings
and his life. In fact, he began with " Pickwick "
to introduce these " curious little nooks " and
" queer old places." Indeed, he lived in Furnival's
Inn when first married, and there wrote the most
of the " Boz " sketches as well as " Pickwick."

Clifford's Inn, too, now on the eve of departure,
is also a reminder of " Pickwick." One, " a tenant
of a ' top set,' was a bad character — shut himself
in his bedroom closet and took a dose of arsenic,"
as is told in " Pickwick," Chapter XXI.

To " Mr. Perker's chambers," in Gray's Inn, —
which still endures as one of the four great Inns
of Court, — went Mr. Pickwick one afternoon, to
find no one at home but the laundress. In Holborn Court, in Gray's Inn, lived also Traddles and
his bride.

Pip was quartered in Barnard's Inn, called by
him a " dingy collection of shabby buildings."

The Temple has ever been prolific in suggestion
to the novelist, and Dickens, like most others who
have written of London life, has made liberal use
of it in " Barnaby Rudge," in " The Tale of Two
Cities," and in many other of his novels.

Staple Inn, at " Holborn Bars," is perhaps the
most quaint and unmodern of any considerable struc-

ture in all London. Mr. Grewgious and Mr. Tartar lived here; also Landless, who occupied "some attic rooms in a corner," and here Mr. Snagsbys was wont to ramble in this old-world retreat.

The "little hall," with "a little lantern in its roof," and its weathercock, is still there, and the stroller down that most businesslike thoroughfare, known in its various continuations as "High Holborn," "Holborn Bars," and "Holborn Viaduct," will find it difficult to resist the allurements of the crazy old timbered frontage of Staple Inn, with its wooden gateway and tiny shops, looking for all the world like a picture from out of an old book.

In Bishop's Court, leading from Chancery Lane, was Crook's rag and bottle shop, where its owner met so ghastly a death. A court to the back of this shop, known as "Chichester Rents," harboured a public house called by Dickens "Sol's Arms." To-day it exists as the "Old Ship," if supposedly authoritative opinion has not erred.

Took's Court is to-day unchanged. Dickens was pleased to call it "Cook's Court." By some it has been called dirty and dingy; it is hardly that, but it may well have been a more sordid looking place in days gone by. At any rate, it was a suitable enough environment for Snagsbys, identified to-day as the stationer's shop next the Imperial Chambers.

As vivid a reminiscence as any is that of the old debtors' prison of Marshalsea. The institution was a court of law and a prison as well, and was first established in 1376 for the determination of causes and differences among the king's menials; and was under the control of the knight marshal, hence its name. Later this court had particular cognizance of murders and other offences committed within the king's court; and here also were committed persons guilty of piracies.

In 1381 the Kentish rebels "broke down the houses of the Marshalsea and the King's Bench in Southwark," and in 1593 "a dangerous insurrection arose in Southwark, owing to the attempt of one of the knight marshal's men to serve a warrant upon a feltmaker's apprentice."

At this time the inhabitants of Southwark complained that "the Knight Marshal's men were very unneighbourly and disdainful among them," with every indication that a prolonged insurrection would endure. However, the matter was brought to the attention of the lord chamberlain, and such edict went forth as assured the inhabitants of the borough freedom from further annoyance. The old gaol building was purchased in 1811 by the government, and at that time refitted as a prison for debtors.

" The entrance gate fronts the High Street near St. George's Church, and a small area leads to the keeper's house. Behind it is a brick building, the ground floor of which contains fourteen rooms in a double row, and three upper stories, each with the same number. They are about ten and a half feet square by eight and a half feet high, and are with boarded floors, a glazed window, and fireplace in each, for male debtors. Nearly adjoining to this is a detached building called the ' Tap,' which has on the ground floor a wine and beer room. The upper story has three rooms for female debtors, similar to those for men. At the extremity of this prison is a small courtyard and building for admiralty prisoners, and a chapel."

The above description, taken from Allen's " History and Antiquities of Southwark," must synchronize with the appearance of the Marshalsea at the time of which Dickens wrote concerning it in " Little Dorrit," based, of course, upon his personal knowledge of the buildings and their functions when the elder Dickens was imprisoned therein in 1822, and the family were living in mean quarters in near-by Lant Street, whither they had removed from Gower Street, North, in order to be near the prison.

Until quite recently it is possible that certain por-

tions of the old Marshalsea were still standing,
though as a prison it was abolished in 1841, but,
with the opening of one of those municipal pleasure
grounds, — one cannot call them gardens, being
merely a flagged courtyard, — the last vestiges are
supposed to have disappeared from general view.
Indeed, it appears that Dickens himself was not
aware of any visible portions of the old building
still remaining. This assertion is based on the following lines taken from the preface of " Little Dorrit : "

" I found the outer front courtyard metamor-
phosed into a butter-shop; and then I almost gave
up every brick for lost. . . . I then came to Marshalsea Place; . . . and whoever goes here will find
his feet on the very paving-stones of the extinct
Marshalsea Gaol, — will see its narrow yard to the
right and to the left but very little altered, if at all,
except that the walls were lowered when the place
got free."

When the elder Dickens was carried to prison,
like Mr. Dorrit, he was lodged in the top story but
one, in the chamber afterward occupied by the Dor-
rits, when Charles, it was said, went often (before
the family removed across the river) to visit him,
crossing presumably the old picturesque London
Bridge. In " David Copperfield," it is evidently

the same edifice which is disguised as the "King's Bench Prison."

In the immediate neighbourhood of the Marshalsea was St. George's Vestry, where, on the cushions, with the church register for a pillow, slept Little Dorrit on the night on which she was shut out of the prison.

Opposite, on High Street, stood until recently the little pie-shop, where Flora read out her lecture to Little Dorrit. Near by, also, was Mr. Cripple's dancing academy. (Deliciously Dickenesque—that name.) Guy's — reminiscent of Bob Sawyer — is but a stone's throw away, as also Lant Street, where he had his lodgings. Said Sawyer, as he handed his card to Mr. Pickwick: "There's my lodgings; it's near Guy's, and handy for me, you know, — a little distance after you've passed St. George's Church; turns out of High Street on right-hand side the way." Supposedly the same humble rooms — which looked out upon a pleasant prospect of a timber-yard — in which lived the Dickens family during the elder Dickens' imprisonment.

In Horsemonger Lane, which runs out of the High Street, was the tobacco-shop of Mrs. Chivery. In the High Street, too, was the old " White Hart " of Sam Weller and even Jack Cade. "The George," "The Spur," "The Queen's Head," and

"The King's Head"—all reminiscent of Dickens—were also here in the immediate neighbourhood. Crossing the river northward, one may retrace their steps toward St. Paul's, near which, a quarter of a century back, might have been seen the arcaded entrance to Doctors' Commons, an institution described by Sam Weller, and which, among other functions, formerly kept guard of all the wills probated in London. The building has since disappeared, and the erstwhile valuable documents removed to Somerset House.

Beyond the "Bank" is Leadenhall Street, where in St. Mary Axe, Dickens had located Pubsey and Co. The firm was domiciled in an "old, yellow, overhanging, plaster-fronted house," and, if it ever existed out of Dickens' imagination, has given way to a more modern and substantial structure.

Fenchurch Street and Mincing Lane are not far away. In the latter was "Chicksey, Veneering, and Stobbles" Counting-House, and still further on Trinity House and Tower Hill to remind one of the locale of certain scenes in "Our Mutual Friend."

In the Minories, leading from Tower Hill, was until recently the "Little Wooden Midshipman" of "Dombey and Son," standing over the door at Messrs. Norie and Wilson's, the nautical publishers. From Tower Hill, whither would one go but through

the Ratcliffe Highway, now St. George's Street,
whereby is suggested the nocturnal wanderings of
"The Uncommercial Traveller." Wapping, Shadwell, and Stepney, with its famous waterside church,
are all redolent of the odours of the sea and reminiscence of Dickens' characters.

Somewhere between here and Limehouse Hole
was Brig Place, not discoverable to-day, where lived
the genial one-armed "Cuttle."

Limehouse, with its "Reach" and "foul and
furtive boats," is closely connected with the personality of Dickens himself, having been the residence
of his godfather, one Huffam, a rigger employed in
a waterside shipyard. What wonder then that the
fascination of riverside London fell early upon the
writer of novels?

At the gate of Limehouse Church, Rokesmith
lay in wait, on murder intent, and all Limehouse
is odorous with memories of riverside crime and
such nefarious deeds as were instigated by Hexham
and Riderhood, an incident suggested, it is said by
Dickens' biographer Forster, by the novelist having seen, in one of his walks in the neighbourhood,
a placard on the hoardings announcing that a body
of a person had been

FOUND DROWNED.

LIMEHOUSE CHURCH.

A neighbouring public house, "The Two Brewers," is supposed to be the original of that referred to by Dickens as "The Six Jolly Fellowship Porters," "a dropsical old house," as he called it, like so many old-world houses, all but falling down, if judged by appearances, but actually not in the least danger of it.

One topic crops up in the notes and queries columns of the literary papers every once and again, viz., the location of the "filthy graveyard" of "Bleak House." It has been variously placed in the churchyard of St. Dunstan's-in-the-West, St. Bartholomew-the-Less, and again in Drury Lane Court, now disappeared. Most likely it was the latter, if any of these neighbourhoods, though it is all hearsay now, though formerly one of the "stock sights" of the "Lady Guide Association," who undertook to gratify any reasonable whim of the inquisitive American.

A recent foregathering of members of the "Boz Club" at Rochester, which celebrated the thirty-first anniversary of the novelist's death on June 9, 1870, occurred in the homely "Bull Inn." This little band of devoted "Dickensians" contained among them Mr. Henry Dickens, K. C., the son of the novelist; Mr. Percy Fitzgerald, who had the honour of being intimately associated with Dickens on *Household Words;* Mr. Luke Fildes, R. A., among whose many famous paintings is that pathetic story-telling canvas, "The Empty Chair," being a reproduction of that portion of Dickens' study at Gad's Hill, wherein stood the writer's desk and chair.

On such a day as that on which the immortal Pickwick "bent over the balustrades of Rochester Bridge contemplating nature and waiting for breakfast," the club (in June, 1903) had journeyed to Rochester to do homage to the fame of their master. The mediæval, cramped High Street, "full of gables, with old beams and timbers carved into strange faces," seems to bask and grow sleepier than ever in the glaring sunlight. It is all practically just as Dickens saw it for the last time three days before his death, as he stood against the wooden palings near the Restoration House contemplating the old Manor House — just the same even to "the queer old clock that projects over the pavement out of a grave red-brick building, as if Time carried on business there, and hung out his sign." Those of the visitors so "disposed" had lunch in the coffee-room of the "Bull," unchanged since the days of the original Pickwickians, but it is only in fancy and framed presentments that one now sees the "G. C. M. P. C." and his disciples, Messrs.

Tupman, Snodgrass, Winkle, and Jingle. So closely, however, do we follow in the footsteps of Mr. Pickwick (wrote a member of the party) that we look through the selfsame coffee-room blinds at the passengers in the High Street, in which entertaining occupation we were disturbed, as was Mr. Pickwick, by the coming of the waiter (perhaps one should say a waiter, not *the* waiter) to announce that the carriages are ready — " an announcement which the vehicles themselves confirm by forthwith appearing before the coffee-room blinds aforesaid."

" ' Bless my soul !' said Mr. Pickwick, as they stood upon the pavement while the coats were being put in. ' Bless my soul ! who's to drive? I never thought of that.'

" ' Oh ! you, of course,' said Mr. Tupman.

" ' I !' exclaimed Mr. Pickwick.

" ' Not the slightest fear, sir,' interposed the hostler.

" ' He don't shy, does he?' inquired Mr. Pickwick.

" ' Shy, sir? — He wouldn't shy if he was to meet a vaggin-load of monkeys with their tails burnt off.' "

The ruined castle and the cathedral are visited, the castle looking more than ever " as if the rooks and daws had picked its eyes out." Before the cathedral, as Mr. Grewgious did before us, we stand for a contemplative five minutes at the great west door of the gray and venerable pile.

"'Dear me,' said Mr. Grewgious, peeping in, ' it's like look-ing down the throat of Old Time.'

"Old Time heaved a mouldy sigh from tomb and arch and vault; and gloomy shadows began to deepen in corners; and damps began to rise from green patches of stone; and jewels, cast upon the pavement of the nave from stained-glass by the declining sun, began to perish."

Or, to quote the more genial Jingle:

"Old Cathedral, too — earthly smell — pilgrims' feet worn away the old steps — little Saxon doors — confessionals like money takers' boxes at theatres — queer customers those monks — Popes, and Lord Treasurers, and all sorts of old fellows, with great red faces, and broken noses, turning up every day — buff jerkins, too — matchlocks — sarcophagus — fine place — old legends too — strange stories, too; capital."

DISAPPEARING LONDON

*P*LACE names are always of interesting origin, in fact, all proper names have a fascination for the historian and litterateur alike. Dickens himself was fond enough of the unusual, and doubtless he made good use of those bygones of a former age, which seemed best to suit his purpose. On the other hand, where would one find in reality such names as Quilp, Cheeryble, Twist, Swiveller, Heep, Tulkinghorn, or Snodgrass? Where indeed! except in the Boston (U. S. A.) Directory? Here will be found Snodgrass and Twist and even a Heep, though he spells it Heap. It would be still further interesting to know the derivation of the names of these individuals; but inasmuch as it would probably throw no additional light on Dickens' own personality, it is passed by without further comment. It is not that these names are any more unusual than many that really do exist, and possibly they all may have had a real entity outside of the author's brain;

still it does represent a deal of thought that each
and every character throughout all of Dickens'
works should seem so singularly appropriate and in
keeping with their names.

With place names Dickens took another line.
Occasionally he played upon a word, though often
he did not disguise it greatly; nor did he intend
to. In many more instances, he presented no coun-
terfeit whatever. For picturesqueness and appro-
priateness, in conjunction with the lives of the individuals of which his novels abound, one could
hardly improve on many actual places of which he
wrote.

London street names, in general, may be divided
into two classes: those named for distinguished,
or, for that matter, notorious persons, as Duke
Street, Wellington Street, George Street, Berkley,
Grosvenor, or Bridgewater Squares; or secondly,
those named for topographical or architectural features, both classes of which, in the earlier times
or immediately following the "Great Fire," under-
went no inconsiderable evolution.

In a later day this will perhaps not prove equally
true; remodelling and rearranging of streets and
squares not only changes the topography, but —
aside from the main arteries — names as well are
often changed or suppressed altogether. Since

Dickens' time many spots, which must have been dearly known and beloved of him, have disappeared, and the process is going on apace, until, with the advent of another century, it will doubtless be difficult to recognize any of the localities of a hundred or more years before.

Some remarkable corruptions have been recorded from time to time, such as Candlewick Street into Cannon Street, Cannon Row to Channel Row, and Snore Hill to Snow Hill, all of which are easily enough followed. Strype's Court (after the historian's family) to Tripe Court, or Duck Lane into Duke Street, are not so easy.

Tavern signs, too, are supposed to have undergone similar perversions, not always with euphonious success, as witness the following: " The Bachnals " into " Bag of Nails," " The God Encompasseth Us " into " Goat and Compasses; " both of the former existed in Victorian days, as does the latter at the present time. Many of these old tavern signs are to be seen to-day in the museum at the Guild Hall.

The actual changes of street names are equally curious, when one attempts to follow the connection, which, for a fact, mostly cannot be done. Thus they stand in their modified form, either as an improvement or debasement. Hog Lane, St. Giles, is now

Crown Street; Grub Street is now gloriously named
Milton Street, and Shoreditch Lane becomes Worship Street.

The matter of street lighting is ever one which
appeals to the visitor to a strange city. Curious
customs there be, even to-day, in the city of London,
which have come down from the age which knew
not the gas-jet or the electric globe.

In Dickens' time, it is confident to say that the
" linkman " was not the *rara avis* that he is to-day,
though evidences are still to be noted in residential
Mayfair and Belgravia, and even elsewhere, of the
appurtenances of his trade, referring to the torch-
extinguishers which were attached outside the door-
ways of the more pretentious houses.

As an established trade, link-carrying has been
extinct for nearly a century, but the many extinguishers still to be seen indicate that the custom
died but slowly from the days when the sturdy
Briton, —

> " *Round as a globe and liquored every chink,*
> *Goodly and great, sailed behind his link.*"
> — *Dryden.*

The first street lighted with gas was Pall Mall,
in 1807, and oil was solely used in many streets and
squares as late as 1860.

The old London watchman — the progenitor of

the modern policeman — used to cry out, "Light! Light! hang out your light." Later came enclosed glass lamps or globes, replacing the candles of a former day. These endured variously, as is noted, until very near the time when electric refulgence was beginning to make itself known. On the whole, until recently, London could not have been an exceedingly well-lighted metropolis, and even now there is many a dark court and alley, which would form in itself a fitting haunt for many a lower-class ruffian of the type Dickens was wont to depict.

The mortality among the old inns of Holborn has been very high of late, and still they vanish. "The Black Bull," known well to Dickens, is the last to come under sentence. Its sign, a veritable bull of Bashan, sculptured in black and gold, has been familiar to all who go down to the City in omnibuses. Until recently the old courtyard of the inn might still have been seen, though the galleried buildings which surrounded it were modern. Before Holborn Viaduct was built, the "Black Bull" stood just at the top of Holborn Hill, that difficult ascent which good citizens found too long, and bad ones too short. "Sirrah, you'll be hanged; I shall live to see you go up Holborn Hill," says Sir Sampson Legend to his thriftless son in Congreve's "Love for Love."

But the "Black Bull" has nearer associations for us. It was here that Mrs. Gamp and Betsy Prig nursed Mr. Lewsome through his fever at the expense of John Westlock. When Mrs. Gamp relieved Betsy in the sick-room, the following dialogue occurred: "'Anything to tell afore you goes, my dear?' asked Mrs. Gamp, setting her bundle down inside the door, and looking affectionately at her partner. 'The pickled salmon,' Mrs. Prig replied, 'is quite delicious. I can partick'ler recommend it. Don't have nothink to say to the cold meat, for it tastes of the stable. The drinks is all good.'" To-day the cold meat is represented by the noble animal on the façade of the inn, and it will probably adorn the Guildhall collection of old shop and tavern signs, where the hideous "Bull and Mouth" and "Goose and Gridiron" still look down on the curious.

Of the matter-of-fact realities of London, which, though still existent, have changed since Dickens' day, London Bridge is undergoing widening and rebuilding, which will somewhat change its general aspect, though its environment remains much the same.

Furnival's Inn, where Dickens lived, has disappeared, and Clifford's Inn has just been sold (1903) in the public auction mart, to be removed, with some hideous and unquiet modern office building doubtless destined to take its place.

New transportation schemes, almost without number, are announced. Electric trams, " tubes," and underground subways are being projected in every direction. These perhaps do not change the surface aspect of thing very much, but they are working a marvellous change in the life of the times. The old underground " District " and " Metropolitan " Railways are being " electrified " by the magnanimity (*sic*) of American capital, and St. Paul's Cathedral has been supplied with a costly electric-light plant at the expense of an American multi-millionaire.

The American invasion of typewriters, roll-top desks, and book printing and binding machinery, are marking an era of change and progress in the production of the printed word, and Continental-made motors and automobiles are driving the humble cart-horse from the city streets in no small way.

It now only remains for the development of the project which is to supplant the ungainly though convenient omnibus with an up-to-date service of motor stages, when, in truth, London will have taken on very much of a new aspect.

One of the most recent disappearances is old Holywell Street, of unsavoury reputation, the whilom Booksellers' Row of Dickens' day, a "narrow, dirty lane" which ran parallel with the Strand from St. Clement's-Danes to St. Mary-le-Strand, and was occupied chiefly by vendors of books of doubtful morality. Wych Street, too, in company with Holywell Street, has gone the same way, in favour of the new thoroughfare which is to connect Holborn and the Strand, an enterprise which also has made way with the Clare Market between Lincoln's Inn Fields and the Strand, a locality well known to, and made use of by, Dickens in "The Old Curiosity Shop."

The identical building referred to therein may be in doubt; probably it is, in that Dickens himself repudiated or at least passed a qualifying observation upon the "waste paper store," which popular tradition has ever connected therewith. But one critic — be he expert or not — has connected it somewhat closely with the literary life of the day, as being formerly occupied by one Tessyman, a bookbinder, who was well acquainted with Dickens, Thackeray, and Cruikshank. The literary pilgrim will give up this most sentimental Dickens *relique* with something of the serious pang that one feels when his favourite idol is shattered, when the little overhanging corner building is finally demolished, as it soon

THE (REFUTED) "OLD CURIOSITY SHOP"

will be, if "improvement" goes on at the pace of the last few years hereabouts.

A drawing of this revered building has been included in the present volume, as suggestive of its recorded literary associations.

There is no question but what it is *the relique* of the first rank usually associated with Dickens' London, as witness the fact that there appears always to be some numbers of persons gazing fondly at its crazy old walls.

The present proprietor appears to have met the demand which undoubtedly exists, and purveys souvenirs, prints, drawings, etc., to the Dickens admirers who throng his shop " in season " and out, and from all parts of the globe, with the balance, as usual, in favour of the Americans.

Rumour has it, and it has been said before, that some " collector " (from America, of course) has purchased this humble shrine, and intends to erect it again across the seas, but no verification of this is possible at this writing.

Whether it had any real being in Dickens' story, the enthusiast, in view of the facts, must decide for him or herself.

" And now at length he's brought
Unto fair London City
Where, in Fleet Street,

All those many see 't
That will not believe my ditty."

— *Butler.*

A half-century ago Temple Bar might have been described as a gateway of stone separating the Strand from Fleet Street — the City from the shire. This particular structure was erected from designs by Sir Christopher Wren in 1670, and from that day until long after Dickens' death, through it have passed countless throngs of all classes of society, and it has always figured in such ceremony of state as the comparatively infrequent visits of the sovereign to the City. The invariable custom was to close the gate whenever the sovereign had entered the City, "and at no other time."

The ceremony was simple, but formal: a herald sounds a trumpet — another herald knocks — a parley — the gates are thrown open and the lord mayor, *pro tempo.*, hands over the sword of the City to the sovereign. It was thus in Elizabeth's time, and it had changed but little throughout Victoria's reign.

The present structure is Temple Bar only in name, being a mere guide-post standing in the middle of the roadway; not very imposing, but it serves its purpose. The former structure was removed

in the eighties, and now graces the private park of
an estate at Walthamstow.

For long before it was taken down, its interior
space was leased to " Childs," the bankers, as a
repository or storage-place for their old ledgers.
Thus does the pomp of state make way for the sordidness of trade, and even the wealthy corporation
of the City of London was not above turning a
penny or two as additional revenue.

The following details of Furnival's Inn, which
since Dickens' time has disappeared, are pertinent
at this time.

" Firnivalles Inn, now an Inn of Chancery, but
some time belonging to Sir William Furnival,
Knight," is the introduction to the description given
by Stow in his "Annals." The greater part of
the old inn was taken down in the time of Charles
I., and the buildings remaining in Dickens' day,
principally occupied as lawyers'offices, were of comparatively modern construction. Since, these too,
have disappeared, and there is little to call it to
mind but the location the inn once occupied.

The Gothic hall, with its timber roof, — part of
the original structure (tempo Richard II.), — was
standing as late as 1818, when the entire inn was
rebuilt by one Peto, who it is to be inferred built

the row in which were the lodgings occupied by Dickens.

In the west end of London changes have been none the less rapid than in the east. The cutting through of Northumberland Avenue, from Trafalgar Square to the river, laid low the gardens and mansion of Northumberland House. Of this stately mansion it is said that it looked more like a nobleman's mansion than any other in London. It was built, in about 1600, by the Earl of Northampton, and came into the hands of the Percies in 1642. Stafford House is perhaps the most finely situated mansion in the metropolis, occupying the corner of St. James' and the Green Parks, and presenting four complete fronts, each having its own architectural character. The interior, too, is said to be the first of its kind in London. The mansion was built by the Duke of York, with money lent by the Marquis of Stafford, afterward Duke of Sutherland; but the Stafford family became owners of it, and have spent at least a quarter of a million sterling on the house and its decorations. Apsley House, at the corner of Piccadilly and Hyde Park, is the residence of the Dukes of Wellington, and is closely associated with the memory of *the* duke. The shell of the house, of brick, is old; but stone frontages, enlargements, and decorations were afterward made.

The principal room facing Hyde Park, with seven windows, is that in which the Great Duke held the celebrated Waterloo Banquet, on the 18th of June in every year, from 1816 to 1852.

In the seventeenth century the Strand was a species of country road, connecting the city with Westminster; and on its southern side stood a number of noblemen's residences, with gardens toward the river. The pleasant days are long since past when mansions and personages, political events and holiday festivities, marked the spots now denoted by Essex, Norfolk, Howard, Arundel, Surrey, Cecil, Salisbury, Buckingham, Villiers, Craven, and Northumberland Streets — a very galaxy of aristocratic names.

Again it is reiterated: the names are, for the most part, actually those now given to great hotels which occupy the former sites of these noble mansions.

The residences of the nobility and gentry were chiefly in the western part of the metropolis. In this quarter there have been large additions of handsome streets, squares, and terraces within the last fifty years. First, the district around Belgrave Square, usually called Belgravia. Northeast from this, near Hyde Park, is the older, but still fashionable quarter, comprehending Park Lane and Mayfair. Still farther north is the modern district, sometimes called Tyburnia, being built on the ground adjacent to what once was "Tyburn," the place of public executions. This district, including Hyde Park Square and Westbourne Terrace, early became a favourite place of residence for city merchants. Lying north and northeast from Tyburnia are an extensive series of suburban rows of buildings and detached villas, which are ordinarily spoken of under the collective name, St. John's Wood, Regent's Park forming a kind of rural centre to the group.

New thoroughfares and the need thereof make a wholly new set of conditions, and such landmarks as have survived the stress of time and weather are thoroughly suggestive and reminiscent of the past, and are often the only guide-posts left by which one may construct the surroundings of a former day.

Of this the stranger is probably more observant than the Londoner born and bred. The gloomy, crowded streets — for they are gloomy, decidedly, most of the time during five months of the year — do not suggest to the native emotions as vivid as to the stranger, who, with a fund of reading for his guide, wanders through hallowed ground which is often neglected or ignored by the Londoner himself.

As for the general architectural effect of London as a type of a great city, it is heightened or lowered accordingly as one approves or disapproves of the artistic qualities of soot and smoke. Fogs are the natural accompaniment of smoke, in the lower Thames valley, at least, and the "London particular" — the pea-soup variety — is a thing to be shuddered at when it draws its pall over the city. At such times, the Londoner, or such proportion of the species as can do so, hurries abroad, if only to the Surrey Hills, scarce a dozen miles away, but possessed of an atmosphere as different as day is from night.

Our own Nathaniel Hawthorne it was who wrote, "There cannot be anything else in its way so good in the world as this effect" (of fog and smoke) "on St. Paul's in the very heart and densest tumult of London. It is much better than staring white; the edifice would not be nearly so grand without this drapery of black." Since we are told that the cost of the building was defrayed by a tax on all coals brought into the port of London, it gets its blackness by right. This grime is at all events a well-established fact, which has to be accepted.

Mr. G. A. Sala, a friend and contemporary of

Dickens, also wrote in favour of the smoky chimneys. He says about St. Paul's: "It is really the better for all the incense which all the chimneys since the time of Wren have offered at its shrine, and are still flinging up every day from their foul and grimy censers." As a flower of speech, this is good, but as criticism it is equivalent to saying the less seen of it the better. M. Taine, the French critic, evidently thought otherwise; he wrote of Somerset House:

"A frightful thing is the huge palace in the Strand which is called Somerset House. Massive and heavy piece of architecture, of which the hollows are inked, the porticoes blackened with soot, where in the cavity of the empty court is a sham fountain without water, pools of water on the pavement, long rows of closed windows. What can they possibly do in these catacombs? It seems as if the livid and sooty fog had even befouled the verdure of the parks. But what most offends the eyes are the colonnades, peristyles, Grecian ornaments, mouldings, and wreaths of the houses, all bathed in soot. Poor antique architecture — what is it doing in such a climate?"

To decide what style of architecture prevails in the medley of different periods constituting London is indeed difficult. One authority concludes that the "dark house in the long, unlovely street," of which Tennyson tells, and Mme. de Staël vituperates, covers the greater number of acres. The fact is, each of the districts constituting London as it now is, i. e., Belgravia, Tyburnia, Bayswater, Kensington, Chelsea, etc., has the impress and character of the time of its greatest popularity and fashion and of the class by which it was principally inhabited. It has always been the city's fate to have its past overgrown and stifled by the enthralling energy and life of the present. It is as a hive that has never been emptied of its successive swarms. This is more or less the fate of all towns that live.

The first map of London was published in 1563 by Ralph Ugga; it shows the same main arteries as exist to-day — the Strand, " Chepe," and Fleet. In a later map of 1610, London and Westminster appear as small neighbouring towns with fields around them; Totten Court, a country village; Kensington and Marylebone secluded hamlets; Clerkenwell and St. Gyllis quite isolated from the main city while Chelsey was quite in the wilds.

Even the great devastating fires did not destroy the line of the public highways. After that of 1666 Sir Christopher Wren wished to remodel the town and make it regular, symmetrical, and convenient; but, although he was the prevailing spirit in the rebuilding of London city, and no important building during forty years was erected without his judgment, his plan for regulating and straightening the streets did not take effect. Much of the picturesque quality of the city is owing to its irregularity and the remains of its past. Wren rebuilt no less than sixty churches, all showing great variety of design. St. Paul's, the third Christian church since early Saxon times on the same site, was his masterpiece.

Of his immediate predecessor, Inigo Jones, the Banqueting House in Whitehall, now used as a museum, remains a fragment of the splendid palace designed by him for James I. The classical revival began with Gibbs, when he built St. Martin's-in-the-Fields, whose Greek portico is the best and most perfect Greek example in London, if we except the caryatides of St. Pancras. The brothers Adam also flourished at this time, and introduced grace of line and much artistic skill in domestic establishments which they built in "The Adelphi" and elsewhere. Chambers with Somerset House, and Sir John Soane with the Bank of England, continued the classical traditions, but its full force came with Nash, "the apostle of plaster," who planned the Quadrant and Regent Street, from Carlton House to Regent's Park, and the terraces in that locality, in the tawdry pseudo-classic stuccoed style, applied indiscriminately to churches, shops, and what not. Not till the middle of the nineteenth century did the Gothic revival flourish. Pugin, Britton, and Sir John Barry then became prominent. The last named built the Houses of Parliament.

The demand for originality in street architecture is to be seen in the tall, important blocks of residential flats and new hotels now rising up in every quarter. Not beautiful and in many cases not even intelligible, they are unmistakable signs of the times, showing the process of transformation which is going on rapidly, sweeping away much that is beautiful to meet the requirements of modern life.

London is perhaps never to be doomed to the curse of the sky-scraper, as it is known in America; the results of such an innovation would be too dire to contemplate, but like every other large city, it is under the spell of twentieth century ideas of progress, and the results, a score or more years hence, will, beyond doubt, so change the general aspect and conditions of life that the spirit of the Victorian era in architecture and art will have been dissipated in air, or so leavened that it will be a glorified London that will be known and loved, even better than the rather depressing atmosphere which has surrounded London and all in it during the thirty-five rapid years which have passed since Dickens' death.

Such, in brief, is a survey of the more noticeable architectural and topographical features of London, which are indicating in no mean fashion the effect of Mr. Whistler's dictum: "Other times, other lines."

Of no place perhaps more true than of London, yet, on the other hand, in no other place, perhaps, does the tendency make way so slowly.

THE COUNTY OF KENT

*T*HE country lying between London and
the English Channel is one of the most
varied and diversified in all England.
The "men of Kent" and the "Kentish men" have
gone down in history in legendary fashion. The
Roman influences and remains are perhaps more
vivid here to-day than elsewhere, while Chaucer
has done perhaps more than all others to give the
first impetus to our acquaintanceship with the pleasures of the road.

"The Pilgrim's Way," the old Roman Watling
Street, and the "Dover Road" of later centuries
bring one well on toward the coaching days, which
had not yet departed ere Mr. Pickwick and his
friends had set out from the present "Golden
Cross" Hotel at Charing Cross for "The Bull"
at Rochester.

One should not think of curtailing a pilgrimage
to what may, for the want of a more expressive
title, be termed "Dickens' Kent," without jour-

neying from London to Gravesend, Cobham, Strood, Rochester, Chatham, Maidstone, Canterbury, and Broadstairs. Here one is immediately put into direct contact, from the early works of " Pickwick," " Copperfield," and " Chuzzlewit," to the last unfinished tale of " Edwin Drood."

No end of absorbing interest is to be found in the footsteps of Pickwick and Jingle, and Copperfield and his friend Steerforth.

To-day one journeys, by a not very progressive or up-to-date railway, by much the same route as did Mr. Pickwick and his friends, and reaches the Medway at Strood and Rochester through a grime and gloom which hardly existed in Dickens' time to the same compromising extent that it does to-day. Bricks, mortar, belching chimneys, and roaring furnaces line the route far into the land of hops.

Twenty miles have passed before those quiet scenes of Kentish life, which imagination has led one to expect, are in the least apparent. The route *via* the river towns of Woolwich, Erith, Gravesend, and Dartford, or *via* Lee, Eltham, and Bexley, is much the same, and it is only as the train crosses the Medway at Strood — the insignificant and uninteresting suburb of Rochester — that any environment of a different species from that seen in London itself is to be recognized. The ancient city of Rochester, with its overgrown and significantly busy dockyard appendage of Chatham, is indicative of an altogether different *raison d'être* from what one has hitherto connected the scenes of Dickens' stories. Kent as a whole, even the Kent of Dickens, would require much time to cover, as was taken by the "Canterbury" or even the "Pickwickian" pilgrims, but a mere following, more or less rapidly, of the Dover Road, debouching therefrom to Broadstairs, will give a vast and appreciative insight into the personal life of Dickens as well as the novels whose scenes are here laid.

The first shrine of moment *en route* would be the house at Chalk, where Dickens spent his honeymoon, and lived subsequently at the birth of his son, Charles Dickens, the younger. Gad's Hill follows closely, thence Rochester and Chatham. The pond on which the "Pickwickians" disported themselves on a certain occasion, when it was frozen, is still pointed out at Rochester, and "The Leather Bottle" at Cobham, where Mr. Pickwick and Mr. Winkle made inquiries for "a gentleman by the name of Tupman," is a very apparent reality; and with this one is well into the midst of the Kent country, made famous by Charles Dickens.

Aside from Dickens' later connection with Rochester, or, rather, Gad's Hill Place, there is his early, and erstwhile happy, life at Chatham to be reckoned with. Here, his father being in employment at the dockyard, the boy first went to school, having been religiously and devotedly put through the early stages of the educative process by his mother.

His generally poor health and weakly disposition kept him from joining in the rough games of his schoolmates, and in consequence he found relaxation in the association of books. Indeed, it was at this time that the first seeds of literary ambition took root, with the result that a certain weedy thing, called " A Tragedy," grew up under the title of " Misnar, the Sultan of India," which at least gave the young author fame among his immediate juvenile circle.

At the age of nine, his father left Chatham, and Dickens was removed with the rest of the family to London, where his early pitiful struggles began, which are recorded elsewhere.

There is a peculiar fascination about both the locality and the old residence of Charles Dickens — Gad's Hill Place — which few can resist. Its lofty situation on a ridge between the Thames and the Medway gives Gad's Hill several commanding views, including the busy windings of the latter, where the Dutch fleet anchored in Elizabeth's reign.

The surroundings seem from all times to have been a kind of Mecca to tramps and petty showmen. That Dickens had an irresistible love for this spot would be clear from the following extract from his works:

" I have my eye on a piece of Kentish road, bordered on either side by a wood, and having, on one hand, between the road dust and the trees, a skirting patch of grass. Wild flowers grow in abundance on this spot, and it lies high and airy, with a distant river stealing steadily away to the ocean. . . ."

Gad's Hill Place is a comfortable, old-fashioned, creeper-clad house, built about a century since, and is on the spot mentioned in Shakespeare's " Henry IV." as the scene of the robbery of the travellers. The following extract from a mediæval record book is interesting:

" 1586, September 29th daye, was a thiefe yt was slayne, buried." Again " 1590, Marche the 17th daie, was a thiefe yt was at Gadshill wounded to deathe, called Robert Writs, buried."

The " Falstaff " Inn is nearly opposite Gad's Hill Place, and dates probably from Queen Anne's time. It formerly had an old-fashioned swinging sign, on one side of which was painted Falstaff and the Merry Wives of Windsor. In its long sanded room there was a copy of Shakespeare's monument in

Westminster Abbey. Fifty years ago about ninety coaches passed this inn daily.

In the garden at Gad's Hill Place Dickens had erected a Swiss chalet presented to him by Fechter, the actor. Here he did his writing "up among the branches of the trees, where the birds and butterflies fly in and out."

The occupiers of Gad's Hill Place since the novelist's death have been Charles Dickens, the younger, Major Budden, and latterly the Honourable F. W. Latham, who graciously opens certain of the apartments to visitors.

In the immediate neighbourhood of Rochester is Cobham, with its famous Pickwickian inn, "The Leather Bottle," where Mr. Tupman sought retirement from the world after the elopement of Miss Wardle with Alfred Jingle.

Dickens himself was very fond of frequenting the inn in company with his friends.

The visitor will have no need to be told that the ancient hostelry opposite the village church is the "Leather Bottle" in question, so beloved of Mr. Pickwick, since the likeness of that gentleman, painted vividly and in the familiar picturesque attitude, on the sign-board, loudly proclaims the fact. It should be one of the fixed *formulæ* of the true Dickensian faith that all admirers of his immortal hero should turn in at the " Leather Bottle " at Cobham, and do homage to Pickwick in the well-known parlour, with its magnificent collection of Dickens relics, too numerous to enumerate here, but of great and varied interest, the present proprietor being himself an ardent Dickens enthusiast.

Here is a shrine, at once worthy, and possessed of many votive offerings from all quarters.

Dickens' personality, as evinced by many of his former belongings, which have found a place here, pervades the bar parlour. So, too, has the very spirit and sentiment of regard for the novelist made the " Leather Bottle's " genial host a marked man. He will tell you many anecdotes of Dickens and his visits here in this very parlour, when he was living at Higham.

The " mild and bitter," or the " arf and arf," is to-day no less pungent and aromatic than when Dickens and his friends regaled themselves amid the same surroundings.

It should be a part of the personal experience of every Dickens enthusiast to journey to the " unspoilt " village of Cobham and spend a half-day beneath the welcoming ' roof of the celebrated " Leather Bottle."

The great love of Dickens for Rochester, the sensitive clinging to the scenes of that happy, but all too short childhood at Chatham, forms an instance of the magnetic power of early associations.

"I have often heard him say," said Forster, "that in leaving the neighbourhood of Rochester he was leaving everything that had given his early life its picturesqueness or sunshine."

What the Lake District is to Wordsworthians, Melrose to lovers of Scott, and Ayr to Burns, Rochester and its neighbourhood is to Dickens enthusiasts throughout the English-speaking world.

The very subtlety of the spell in the former cases holds aloof many an average mortal who grasps at once the home thrusts, the lightly veiled satire, the poor human foibles, fads, and weaknesses in the characters of Dickens. The ordinary soul, in whom the "meanest flower that grows" produces no tears, may possibly be conscious of a lump in his throat as he reads of the death of Jo or Little Nell. The deaths of Fagin and Bill Sikes are, after all, a more native topic to the masses than the final exit of Marmion.

Not only so, but the very atmosphere of the human abodes, to say nothing of minute and readily identified descriptions of English scenery, permeates the stories of Dickens.

Gad's Hill at Higham can, to be sure, hardly be reckoned as a London suburb, but on the other hand it was, in a way, merely a suburban residence near enough thereto to be easily accessible.

Even in his childhood days Dickens had set his heart upon the possession of this house, which was even then known as Gad's Hill Place. His father, who at that time had not fallen upon his unfortunate state, had encouraged him to think that it might be possible, " when he should have grown to a man," did he but work hard.

At any rate Dickens was able to purchase the estate in 1856, and from that date, until his death in 1870, it was occupied by him and his family. Writing to Forster at this time, Dickens stated that he had just " paid the purchase-money for Gad's Hill Place" (£1,790). How Dickens' possession of the house actually came about is told in his own words, in a letter written to his friend, M. De Cerjet, as follows:

" I happened to be walking past (the house) a year or so ago, with my sub-editor of *Household Words* (Mr. W. H. Wills), when I said to him: ' You see that house? It has always a curious interest for me, because when I was a small boy down in these parts, I thought it the most beautiful house (I suppose because of its famous old cedar-trees) ever seen. And my poor father used to bring me to look at it, and used to say that if ever I grew up to be a clever man perhaps I might own that house, or such another house. In remembrance of which, I have always, in passing, looked to see if it was to be sold or let, and it has never been to me like any other house, and it has never changed at all.' We came back to town and my friend went out to dinner. Next morning he came to me in great excitement, and said, ' It is written that you are to have that house at Gad's Hill. The lady I had allotted to take down to dinner yesterday began to speak of that neighbourhood. " You know it?" I said; " I have been there to-day." " Oh, yes," she said, " I know it very well; I was a child there in the house they call Gad's Hill Place. My father was the rector, and lived there many years. He has just died, has left it to me, and I want to sell it." So,' says the sub-editor, ' you must buy it, now or never!' I did, and hope to pass next summer there."

It is difficult to regard the numerous passages descriptive of places in Dickens' books without reverence and admiration. The very atmosphere appears, by his pen, to have been immortalized.

Even the incoherences of Jingle have cast a new cloak of fame over Rochester's Norman Cathedral and Castle!

" ' Ah! fine place, glorious pile — frowning

DICKENS' STUDY AT GAD'S HILL PLACE.

From a painting by Luke Fildes, R. A.

walls — tottering arches — dark nooks — crumbling staircases. Old Cathedral too — earthy smell — pilgrims' feet wore away the old steps — little Saxon doors — confessionals like money-takers' boxes at theatres — queer customers those monks — Popes and Lord Treasurers and all sorts of fellows, with great red faces and broken noses, turning up every day — buff jerkins too — matchlocks — sarcophagus — fine place — old legends too — strange stories : capital,' and the stranger continued to soliloquize until they reached the Bull Inn, in the High Street, where the coach stopped."

A further description of the Cathedral by Dickens is as follows :

" A certain awful hush pervades the ancient pile, the cloisters, and the churchyard, after dark, which not many people care to encounter. The cause of this is not to be found in any local superstition that attaches to the precincts, but it is to be sought in the innate shrinking of dust with the breath of life in it from dust out of which the breath of life has passed; also in the . . . reflection, ' If the dead do, under any circumstances, become visible to the living, these are such likely surroundings for the purpose that I, the living, will get out of them as soon as I can.' "

With Durdles and Jasper, from the pages of

" Edwin Drood," also, one can descend into the crypt of the earlier Norman church, the same they visited by moonlight, when Durdles kept tapping the wall " just where he expected to disinter a whole family of ' old 'uns.' "

In numerous passages Dickens has truly immortalized what perforce would otherwise have been very insignificant and unappealing structures. The Bull Inn, most interesting of all, is unattractive enough as a hostelry. It would be gloomy and foreboding in appearance indeed, and not at all suggestive of the cheerful house that it is, did it but lack the association of Dickens.

No. 17 in the inn is the now famous bedroom of Mr. Pickwick, and the present coffee-room now contains many relics of Dickens purchased at the sale held at Gad's Hill Place after the author's death.

Chatham Lines, the meadows, the Cathedral and Castle, " Eastgate House," the Nuns' House of " Edwin Drood," " Restoration House," the " Satis House " of " Great Expectations," serve in a way to suggest in unquestionable manner the debt which Dickens laid upon Rochester and its surroundings.

" Eastgate House " is said to be the original of the home of Mr. Sapsea, the auctioneer and estate agent in " Edwin Drood."

The date of Eastgate House, 1591, is carved on

a beam in one of the upper rooms. Dickens, in
" Edwin Drood," alludes to Eastgate House as follows :

" In the midst of Cloisterham [Rochester] stands
the ' Nuns' House,' a venerable brick edifice, whose
present appellation is doubtless derived from the
legend of its conventual uses. On the trim gate
enclosing its old courtyard is a resplendent brass
plate, flashing forth the legend: ' Seminary for
young ladies: Miss Twinkleton.' The house-front
is so old and worn, and the brass plate is so shining
and staring, that the general result has reminded
imaginative strangers of a battered old beau with
a large modern eye-glass stuck in his left eye."

To-day there is noticeable but little change, and
the charm of Rochester in literary association, if
only with respect to Dickens, is far greater than
many another city greater and more comprehensive
in its scope.

In the opening scenes of the earlier work Dickens treated of Rochester, but the whole plot of his
last novel, " Edwin Drood," is centred in the same
city.

" For sufficient reasons, which this narrative
[" Edwin Drood "] will itself unfold as it advances,
a fictitious name must be bestowed upon the old
Cathedral town. Let it stand in these pages as

Cloisterham. It was once possibly known to the Druids by another name, and certainly to the Romans by another; and a name more or less in the course of many centuries can be of little moment in its dusty chronicles." Dickens describes it thus:

" An ancient city, Cloisterham, and no meet dwelling-place for any one with hankerings after the noisy world. A monotonous, silent city, deriving an earthy flavour throughout from its cathedral crypt, and so abounding in vestiges of monastic graves that the Cloisterham children grow small salad in the dust of abbots and abbesses, and make dirt-pies of nuns and friars; while every ploughman in its outlying fields renders to once puissant Lord Treasurers, Archbishops, Bishops, and such like, the attention which the Ogre in the story-book desired to render to his unbidden visitor, and grinds their bones to make his bread. . . . In a word, a city of another and a bygone time is Cloisterham, with its hoarse Cathedral bell, its hoarse rooks hovering about the Cathedral tower, its hoarser and less distinct rooks in the stalls far beneath."

For the Dickens pilgrim, the first landmark that will strike his eye will be the Corn Exchange, " with its queer old clock that projects over the pavement " (" Edwin Drood "). Watts' Charity, a triple-gabled edifice in the High Street, has become

world-famous through Dickens' " Christmas Story."
" Strictly speaking," he says, " there were only six
poor travellers, but being a traveller myself, and
being withal as poor as I hope to be, I brought the
number up to seven."

The building is to be recognized both by the
roof angles and the inscriptions on the walls, the
principal one of which runs thus:

> RICHARD WATTS ESQ.,
>
> *by his Will, dated 22 Aug. 1579,*
> *founded this Charity*
> *for Six poor Travellers,*
> *who not being Rogues or Proctors*
> *may receive gratis for one night,*
> *Lodging, Entertainment,*
> *and Fourpence each.*

Could good Richard Watts come forth some
morning from his resting-place in the south transept
over the way, he would have the pleasure of seeing
how efficiently the trustees are carrying on their
work.

The visitor, too, who desires to see the prepara-
tion for the coming evening's guests, may calculate
on being no less " curtuoslie intreated " than the
guests proper. In the little parlour to the left, as
we enter from the street door, is the famous book

containing the names and signatures of numerous celebrities whose curiosity has led them hither — Dickens, Wilkie Collins, and J. L. Toole amongst the number. From the kitchen is served out the meat for the supper, which consists of half a pound of beef, a pint of coffee, and half a loaf for each poor traveller.

In the south transept of Rochester Cathedral is a plain, almost mean, brass to Charles Dickens:

"CHARLES DICKENS.   Born at Portsmouth, seventh of February, 1812.

"Died at Gadshill Place, by Rochester, ninth of June, 1870.

"Buried in Westminster Abbey.   To connect his memory with the scenes in which his earliest and latest years were passed, and with the associations of Rochester Cathedral and its neighbourhood, which extended over all his life, this tablet, with the sanction of the Dean and Chapter, is placed by his Executors."

This recalls the fact that the great novelist left special instructions in his will: *"I conjure my friends on no account to make me the subject of any monument, memorial, or testimonial whatever. I rest my claims to the remembrance of my country upon my published works."*

It was in this transept that Charles Dickens was to have been laid to rest.   The grave, in fact, had been dug, and all was ready, when a telegram came

deciding that Westminster Abbey, and not Rochester, should be the long last home of the author.

Great interest attaches itself to Broadstairs,
where Dickens lived upon returning from his journey abroad in company with his wife and " Phiz,"
in 1851. " Bleak House " is still pointed out here,
and is apparently revered with something akin to
sentiment if not of awe.

As a matter of fact, it is not the original of
" Bleak House " at all, that particular edifice being
situate in Hertfordshire, near St. Albans.

This is an excellent illustration of the manner
in which delusive legends grow up on the smallest
foundations. On the cliff overlooking the little pier
and close to the coast-guard station, stands Fort
House, a tall and very conspicuous place which
Charles Dickens rented during more than one summer. This is now known as Bleak House because,
according to a tradition on which the natives posi-
tively insist, " Bleak House" was written there.
Unfortunately for the legend, it is the fact that,
although " Bleak House " was written in many
places, — Dover, Brighton, Boulogne, London, and
where not, — not a line of it was written at Broadstairs.

Dickens' own description of Broadstairs was, in
part, as follows:

"Half awake and half asleep, this idle morning
in our sunny window on the edge of a chalk cliff
in the old-fashioned watering-place to which we
are a faithful resorter, we feel a lazy inclination to
sketch its picture.

"The place seems to respond. Sky, sea, beach,
and village, lie as still before us as if they were
sitting for the picture. But the ocean lies winking
in the sunlight like a drowsy lion — its glassy
waters scarcely curve upon the shore — the fishing-
boats in the tiny harbour are all stranded in the
mud — our two colliers (our watering-place has a
maritime trade employing that amount of shipping)
have not an inch of water within a quarter of a mile
of them, and turn, exhausted, on their sides, like
faint fish of an antediluvian species. Rusty cables
and chains, ropes and rings, undermost parts of
posts and piles and confused timber defences against
the waves, lie strewn about, in a brown litter of
tangled seaweed and fallen cliff.

"In truth, our watering-place itself has been left
somewhat high and dry by the tide of years. Concerned as we are for its honour, we must reluc-
tantly admit that the time when this pretty little
semi-circular sweep of houses tapering off at the
end of the wooden pier into a point in the sea, was
a gay place, and when the lighthouse overlooking

it shone at daybreak on company dispersing from
public balls, is but dimly traditional now. There
is a ' bleak chamber' in our watering-place which
is yet called the Assembly ' Rooms.' . . .

". . . We have a church, by the bye, of course
— a hideous temple of flint, like a great petrified
haystack. . . .

"Other population than we have indicated, our
watering-place has none. There are a few old used-
up boatmen who creep about in the sunlight with
the help of sticks, and there is a poor imbecile shoemaker who wanders his lonely life away among
the rocks, as if he were looking for his reason —
which he will never find. Sojourners in neighbouring watering-places come occasionally in flys to
stare at us, and drive away again.

". . . And since I have been idling at the window here, the tide has risen. The boats are dancing
on the bubbling water : the colliers are afloat again;
the white-bordered waves rush in; the children —

> " ' Do chase the ebbing Neptune, and do fly him
> When he comes back;'

the radiant sails are gliding past the shore, and
shining on the far horizon; all the sea is sparkling,
heaving, swelling up with life and beauty, this
bright morning." ("Our Watering-Place.")

Another reference of Dickens to the Kent coast was in one of the *Household Words* articles, entitled "Out of Season." The Watering-Place "out of season" was Dover, and the place without a cliff was Deal.

Writing to his wife of his stay there, he says: "I did nothing at Dover (except for *Household Words*), and have not begun 'Little Dorrit,' No. 8, yet. But I took twenty-mile walks in the fresh air, and perhaps in the long run did better than if I had been at work."

One can hardly think of Deal or Dover without calling to mind the French coast opposite, often, of a clear day, in plain view.

In spite of Dickens' intimacies with the land of his birth, he had also a fondness for foreign shores, as one infers from following the scope of his writings.

Of Boulogne, he writes in " Our French Watering-Place" (*Household Words*, November 4, 1854):

" Once solely known to us as a town with a very long street, beginning with an abattoir and ending with a steamboat, which it seemed our fate to behold only at daybreak on winter mornings, when (in the days before continental railroads), just sufficiently awake to know that we were most uncomfortably asleep, it was our destiny always to clatter through it, in the coupé of the diligence from Paris, with a sea of mud behind, and a sea of tumbling waves before."

An apt and true enough description that will be recognized by many. Continuing, he says, also truly enough:

"But our French watering-place, when it is once got into, is a very enjoyable place."

To those to whom these racy descriptions appeal, it is suggested that they familiarize themselves with the "Reprinted Pieces," edited by Charles Dickens the younger, and published in New York in 1896, a much more complete edition, with explanatory notes, than that which was issued in London.

THE RIVER THAMES

Glide gently, thus for ever glide,
O Thames! that other bards may see
As lovely visions by thy side
As now, fair river! come to me.
O glide, fair stream, for ever so,
Thy quiet soul on all bestowing,
Till all our minds for ever flow
As thy deep waters now are flowing.

WORDSWORTH...

*E*VER present in the minds and hearts of the true Londoner is the "majestic Thames;" though, in truth, while it is a noble stream, it is not so all-powerful and mighty a river as romance would have us believe.

From its source, down through the Shires, past Oxford, Berks, and Bucks, and finally between Middlesex, Surrey, and Essex, it ambles slowly but with dignity. From Oxford to Henley and Cookham, it is at its best and most charming stage. Passing Maidenhead, Windsor, Stains, Richmond, Twickenham, and Hammersmith, and reaching Putney Bridge, it comes into London proper, after having journeyed on its gladsome way through green fields and sylvan banks for a matter of some hundred and thirty miles.

At Putney Bridge and Hammersmith is the centre of the fishing section, and this was the background depicted by the artist who drew the wrapper for the first serial issue of " The Posthumous Papers of the Pickwick Club." Putney Church is seen in the distance, with its Henry VIII. Chapel, and in the foreground Mr. Pickwick is found dozing in his traditional punt, — that curious box, or coffin-like, affair, which, as a pleasure craft, is apparently indigenous to the Thames.

Above this point the river is still:

> . . . " *The gentle Thames*
> *And the green, silent pastures yet remain.*"

Poets have sung its praises, and painters extolled its charms. To cite Richmond alone, as a locality, is to call up memories of Sir Joshua Reynolds, Walpole, Pope, Thomson, and many others whose names are known and famed of letters and art.

Below, the work-a-day world has left its stains and its ineffaceable marks of industry and grime, though it is none the less a charming and fascinating river, even here in its lower reaches. And here, too, it has ever had its literary champions. Was not Taylor — " the water poet " — the Prince of Thames Watermen? "

If swans are characteristic of the upper reaches, the waterman or the bargeman, assuredly, is of the lower. With the advent of the railway, — which came into general use and effective development during Dickens' day, — it was popularly supposed that the traffic of the " silent highway " would be immeasurably curtailed. Doubtless it was, though the real fact is, that the interior water-ways of Britain, and possibly other lands, are far behind *" la belle France "* in the control and development of this means of intercommunication.

There was left on the Thames, however, a very considerable traffic which — with due regard for vested rights, archaic by-laws and traditions, " customs of the port," and other limitations without number — gave, until very late years, a livelihood to a vast riverside population.

The change in our day from what it was, even in the latter days of Dickens' life, is very marked. New bridges — at least a half-dozen — have been built, two or three new tunnels, steam ferries, — of a sort, — and four railway bridges; thus the aspect of the surface of the river has perforce changed considerably, opening up new vistas and *ensembles* formerly unthought of.

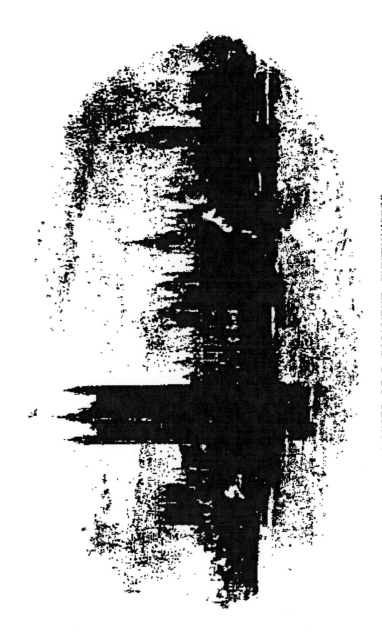

HOUSES OF PARLIAMENT, WESTMINSTER.

Coming to London proper, from "Westminster" to the "Tower," there is practically an inexhaustible store of reminiscence to be called upon, if one would seek to enumerate or picture the sights, scenes, and localities immortalized by even the authors contemporary with Dickens.

Not all have been fictionists, — a word which is used in its well meant sense, — some have been chroniclers, like the late Sir Walter Besant and Joseph Knight, whose contributions of historical résumé are of the utmost value. Others are mere "antiquarians" or, if you prefer, historians, as the author of "London Riverside Churches." Poets there have been, too, who have done their part in limning its charms, from Wordsworth's "Westminster Bridge," on the west, written at the beginning of the nineteenth century, to "A White-Bait Dinner at Greenwich," of Peacock, or "The Boy at the Nore," of Tom Hood, on the east.

When, in the forties, the new Parliament Houses were approaching their completed form, a new feature came into the prospect.

As did Wren, the architect of St. Paul's, so did Barry, the architect of the Parliament Buildings, come in for many rough attacks at the hands of statesmen or Parliamentarians, who set their sails chiefly to catch a passing breath of popular applause, in order that they might provide for themselves a niche or a chapter in the history of this grand building.

It was claimed that the flanking towers would mix inextricably with those of St. Margaret's and the Abbey; that were they omitted, the structure would be dwarfed by the aforesaid churches, — and much more of the same sort. In its present completed form, it is a very satisfying " Tudor-Gothic," or " Gothic-Tudor," building, admirably characteristic of the dignity and power which should be possessed by a great national administrative capitol.

The worst defect, if such be noticeable among its vast array of excellencies, is the unfinished northerly, or up-river, façade.

To recall a reminiscence of Dickens' acquaintance with the locality, it may be mentioned that in Milbank, hard by the Houses of Parliament, is Church Street, running to the river, where Copperfield and Peggotty followed Martha, bent upon throwing herself into the flood.

In Dickens' time, that glorious thoroughfare, known of all present-day visitors to London, the Victoria Embankment, was in a way non-existent. In the forties there was some agitation for a new thoroughfare leading between the western and the eastern cities. Two there were already, one along Holborn, though the later improvement of the Holborn Viaduct more than trebled its efficiency, and the other, the " Royal Route," — since the court gave up its annual state pageant by river, — *via* the Strand, Fleet Street, and Ludgate Hill.

As originally projected, the " Embankment " was to be but a mere causeway, or dyke, running parallel to the shore of the river from Westminster Bridge to Blackfriars, " with ornamental junctions at Hungerford and Waterloo Bridges."

Whatever the virtues of such a plan may have been, practically or artistically, it was ultimately changed in favour of a solid filling which should extend from the fore-shore to somewhat approximating the original river-banks. This left the famous " Stairs " far inland, as stand York Stairs and Essex Stairs to-day.

The result has been that, while it has narrowed the river itself, it has made possible an ample roadway through the heart of a great city, the peer of which does not exist elsewhere. It is to be feared, though, that it is hardly appreciated. The London cabby appears to be fascinated with the glare and intricacy of the Strand, and mostly the drivers of brewers' drays and parcel delivery vans the same. The result is that, but for a few earnest folk who are really desirous of getting to their destination quickly, it is hardly made use of to anything like the extent which it ought.

The Thames in London proper was, in 1850, crossed by but six bridges. Blackfriars Railway Bridge, Charing Cross Railway Bridge, and the Tower Bridge did not come into the *ensemble* till later, though the two former were built during Dickens' lifetime.

Westminster Bridge, from whence the Embankment starts, was the second erected across the Thames. It appears that attempts were made to obtain another bridge over the Thames besides that known as "London Bridge," in the several reigns of Elizabeth. James I., Charles I. and II., and George I.; but it was not until the year 1736 that Parliament authorized the building of a second bridge, namely, that at Westminster. Prior to this date, the only communication between Lambeth and Westminster was by ferry-boat, near Palace Gate, the property of the Archbishop of Canterbury, to whom it was granted by patent under a rent of £20, as an equivalent for the loss of which, on the opening of the bridge, the see received the sum of £2,205.

In 1739, amid great opposition from "The Most Worshipful Company of Watermen," the first stone

was laid, and in 1747 the structure was completed,
the plans having been changed *interim* in favour of
an entire stone structure.

As it then stood Westminster Bridge was 1,066
feet long, or 260 feet shorter than Waterloo Bridge;
its width is 42 feet, height, 58 feet. The proportions of the bridge were stated by an antiquary,
since departed this life, to be "so accurate that,
if a person speak against the wall of any of the
recesses on one side of the way, he may be distinctly heard on the opposite side; even a whisper
is audible during the stillness of the night," a circumstance of itself of little import, one would think,
but which is perhaps worth recording, as indicating
the preciseness of a certain class of historians of
the time. To-day it is to be feared that such details
are accepted, if not with credulity, at least with
indifference.

This fine work not being equal to the demands
which were made upon it, it gave way in 1865 to
the present graceful and larger iron-spanned structure, which, while in no way a grand work of
art, does not offend in any way.

As the "Embankment" passes Charing Cross
Railway Bridge, we are reminded that this rather
ugly structure, with its decidedly ungainly appendage in the form of a huge railway station, did not

exist in Dickens' day. Instead there was a more
or less graceful suspension bridge, known as Hungerford Bridge, which crossed the river from the
lower end of Hungerford Market, now alas replaced by the aforesaid crude railway station, which,
in spite of the indication of progress which it suggests, can hardly be an improvement on what existed on the same site some fifty years ago.

Hungerford Market was a structure occupying
much the same area as the present railway station;
beside it was Warren's Blacking Factory, where
Dickens, as a boy, tied up the pots of the darksome
fluid. Just below was " Hungerford Stairs," another of those riverside landing-places, and one
which was perhaps more made use of than any other
between Blackfriars and Westminster, its aristocratic neighbour, " York Stairs," being but seldom
used at that time. The latter, one of the few existing works of Inigo Jones, remains to-day, set
about with greensward in the " Embankment Gardens," but Hungerford Stairs, like the Market, and
old Hungerford Bridge, has disappeared for ever.
The present railway bridge is often referred to as
Hungerford Bridge, by reason of the fact that a
foot-bridge runs along its side, a proviso made when
the former structure was permitted to be pulled
down. Of the old blacking factory, which must

have stood on the present Villiers Street, nothing remains, nor of its "crazy old wharf, abutting on the water when the tide was out, and literally overrun by rats."

On the 1st of May, 1845, Hungerford Suspension Bridge was opened to the public without ceremony, but with much interest and curiosity, for between noon and midnight 36,254 persons passed over it. Hungerford was at that time the great focus of the Thames Steam Navigation, the embarkation and landing exceeding two millions per annum. The bridge was the work of Sir I. K. Brunel, and was a fine specimen of engineering skill. There were three spans, the central one between the piers being 676 feet, or 110 feet more than the Menai Bridge, and second only to the span of the wire suspension bridge at Fribourg, which is nearly 900 feet. It was built without any scaffolding, with only a few ropes, and without any impediment to the navigation of the river. The entire cost of the bridge was £110,000, raised by a public company.

The bridge was taken down in 1863, and the chains were carried to Clifton for the Suspension Bridge erecting there. The bridge of the South Eastern Railway at Charing Cross occupies the site of the old Hungerford Bridge.

Many novelists, philanthropists, and newspaper

writers have dwelt largely upon the horrors of a
series of subterranean chambers, extending beneath
the Adelphi Terrace in the West Strand, and locally
and popularly known as the "Adelphi Arches."
To this day they are a forbidding, cavernous black
hole, suggestive of nothing if not the horrors of
thievery, or even murder. They are, however, so
well guarded by three policemen on "fixed point"
duty that at night there is probably no more safe
locality in all London than the former unsavoury
neighbourhood, a statement that is herein confidently made by the writer, as based on a daily and
nightly acquaintance with the locality of some years.

Coupled in association with Dickens' reference
to having played round about during his boyhood,
while living in Lant Street, and working in Warren's Blacking Factory, only two blocks away in
Villiers Street, is also the memory of David Copperfield's strange liking for these "dark arches." Originally these yawning crevices were constructed as
a foundation for the "Adelphi Terrace," the home
of the Savage Club, and of Garrick at one time,
and now overlooking the "Embankment Gardens,"
though formerly overhanging the actual river-bank
itself.

What wonder that these catacomb-like vaults
should have been so ghostly reminiscent and sug-

gestive of the terrors associated with the "Jack
Shepards" and "Jonathan Wilds," whose successors
lived in Dickens' day. One very great reality in
connection with its unsavoury reputation is the tun-
nel-like opening leading Strandward. Through this
exit was the back door of a notorious "Coffee and
Gambling House," like enough the "little, dirty,
tumble-down public house" hard by Hungerford
Stairs, where the Micawbers located just before
emigrating, and referred to by Dickens in "David
Copperfield." Through this door persons of too
confiding a disposition were lured by thieves and
blacklegs, drugged, swindled, and thrown out bodily
into the darksome tunnel to recover, if they returned
to consciousness before discovered by the police,
their dazed and befuddled wits as best they might.

"The Adelphi" itself is one of those lovable
backwaters of a London artery, which has only
just escaped spoliation at the hands of the improver.
A few months since it was proposed to raze and
level off the whole neighbourhood as a site for the
municipal offices of the Corporation of the City
of London, but wire-pulling, influence, or what not,
turned the current in another direction, and to-day
there is left in all its original and winsome glory
the famous Adelphi, planned and built by the broth-

ers Adam, as a sort of acropolis as a site for institutions of learning and culture.

In Dickens' time, though the "Embankment" was taking form, it lacked many of those adornments which to-day place it as one of the world's great thoroughfares. Immediately opposite on the fore-shore of the river is the Egyptian obelisk, one of the trio of which another is in the Place de la Concord at Paris, and the other in Central Park, New York. Here it was transferred to a new environment, and since the seventies this pictured monolith of a former civilization has stood amid its uncontemporary surroundings, battered more sorely by thirty years of London's wind and weather than by its ages of African sunshine.

"Billingsgate" was one of the earliest watergates of London, the first on the site having been built in the year 400 B. C., and named after Belin, King of the Britons. The present "Billingsgate Market" is a structure completed in 1870. Since 1699 London's only *entrepot* for the edible finny tribe has been here, with certain rights vested in the ancient "Guild of Fishmongers," without cognizance of which it would not be possible to "obtain by purchase any fish for food."

A stage floats in the river off the market, beside which float all manner of craft, from the humble

BILLINGSGATE.

wherry to the ostentatious puffy little steamers who
collect the cargoes of the North Sea fleet and rush
them to market against all competitors. The market
opens at five A. M., summer and winter. Moored to
a buoy, a short distance from the shore, are always
to be found one or more Dutch fishing-boats, certain inalienable rights permitting "no more than
three " to be at any or all times tied up here. There
is among the native watermen themselves a guarded
jealousy and contempt for these "furriners," and
should the cable once be slipped, no other Dutchman
would ever again be allowed to pick it up. Hence
it is that by traditionary rights one or more of these
curious stub-nosed, broad-beamed craft, like the
Dutch *haus-vrow* herself, are always to be seen.

The Londoner found amusement at Whitsun-
tide in a visit to Greenwich Fair, then an expedition
of far greater importance than in later years, the
journey having to be made by road. The typical
"fish dinner " of Greenwich, as it obtained in the
middle of the last century, was an extraordinary
affair, perhaps the most curious repast which ever
existed in the minds of a culinary genius, or a
swindling hotel-keeper, — for that is about what
they amounted to in the latter days of this popular
function now thankfully past.

Many and varied courses of fish, beginning with

the famous " whitebait," the " little silver stars "
of the poet's fancy, more or less skilfully prepared,
were followed by such gastronomic unconventions
as " Duck and Peas," " Beans and Bacon," and
" Beef and Yorkshire," all arranged with due regard for inculcating an insatiable and expensive
thirst, which was only allayed at the highest prices
known to the *bon vivant* of a world-wide experience.
For many years after Dickens' death in 1870, indeed, until quite recent years, with only occasional
lapses, the " Ministers of the Crown " were wont to
dine at Greenwich, as a fitting *Gargantuan* orgy
to the labours of a brain-racking session.

As one who knows his London has said, you can
get a much better fish dinner, as varied and much
more attractive, in the neighbourhood of Billingsgate, for the modest sum of two shillings.

No mention of London riverside attractions can
be made without enlarging somewhat upon the sordid and unsavoury (in more senses than one) Limehouse Hole and Limehouse Reach.

Redolent of much that is of the under world,
these localities, with indeed those of all the waterside round about, have something of the fascination
and glamour which surrounds a foreign clime itself. Here in " Brig Place," evidently an imaginary
neighbourhood, Dickens placed the genial hook-

armed Cuttle, and he must not only have studied these types upon the spot, but must have been enamoured of the salty sentiment which pervades the whole region from the notorious Ratcliffe Highway on the north, now known by the more respectable name of St. George's Street, made famous in the "Uncommercial Traveller," to the "Stairs" near Marshalsea on the south, where Dickens used to stroll of a morning before he was allowed to visit his father in the prison, and imagine those "astonishing fictions about the wharves and the Tower."

It was at Limehouse, too, that Dickens' godfather, Huffman, a rigger and sailmaker, lived, and with whom Dickens was so fond, when a boy, of making excursions roundabout the "Hole" and the "Reach" with their "foul and furtive boats."

Returning westward one finds, adjoining Somerset House, the famed Waterloo Bridge, great as to its utility and convenience, and splendid as to its appointments. "An exquisite combination of all that is most valuable in bridge architecture," wrote Knight in 1842; called also by Canova, whom of late it is become the custom to decry, the finest bridge in Europe, and worth coming from Rome to see. It is the masterwork of one John Rennie, a Scotch schoolmaster, and was completed in 1817, and named after the decisive event achieved by His Majesty's forces two years before. It has ever been the one short cut into South London from all the west central region, and is the continuation of the roadway across the Strand — Wellington Street — intimately associated with Dickens by the building which formerly contained the offices of *Household Words* and the London chambers of Dickens' later years.

Blackfriars Bridge follows immediately after the Temple Gardens, but, unlike Waterloo or the present London Bridge, is a work so altered and disfigured from what the architect originally intended, as to be but a slummy perversion of an inanimate thing, which ought really to be essentially beautiful and elegant as useful.

At this point was also the *embouchement* of the "Fleet," suggestive of irregular marriages and the Fleet Prison, wherein Mr. Pickwick "sat for his picture," and suffered other indignities.

As Dickens has said in the preface to "Pickwick," "legal reforms have pared the claws by which a former public had suffered." The laws of imprisonment for debt have been altered, and the Fleet Prison pulled down.

A little further on, up Ludgate Hill, though not really in the Thames district, is the "Old Bailey,"

LONDON BRIDGE

eading to "Newgate," whereon was the attack of
the Gordon Rioters so vividly described in Chapter
LXIV. of "Barnaby Rudge." The doorway which
was battered down at the time is now in the possession of a London collector, and various other
relics are continually finding their way into the
salesroom since the entire structure was razed in
1901.

Southwark Bridge, an ordinary enough structure
of stone piers and iron arches, opened another thoroughfare to South London, between Blackfriars
and the incongruous and ugly pillar known as the
Monument, which marks the starting-point of the
great fire of 1666, and is situated on the northerly
end of the real and only "London Bridge" of the
nursery rhyme.

As recorded, it actually did fall down, as the
result of an unusually high tide in 1091. As the
historian of London Bridge has said, "a magnificent bridge is a durable expression of an ideal in
art, whether it be a simple arch across an humble
brook, or a mighty structure across a noble river."

The history of London Bridge is a lengthy account of itself, and the period with which we have
to deal carries but a tithe of the lore which surrounds it from its birth.

It was said by Dion Cassius that a bridge stood

here in the reign of Claudius, but so far into antiquity is this (44 A. D.), that historians in general do not confirm it. What is commonly known as "Old London Bridge," with its houses, its shops, and its chapels, a good idea of which is obtained from the sixth plate of Hogarth's "Marriage à la Mode," was a wonderfully impressive thing in its day, and would be even now, did its like exist.

The structures which roofed the bridge over, as it were, were pulled down; and various reparations made from time to time preserved the old structure until, in 1824, was begun the present structure, from the designs of Rennie, who, however, died before the work was begun. It was opened by William IV. and Queen Adelaide in 1831, and occupies a site two hundred or more feet further up the river than the structure which it replaced, the remains of which were left standing until 1832. Thus it is likely enough that Dickens crossed and re-crossed this famous storied bridge, many times and oft, when his family was living in Lant Street, in Southwark, while the father of the family was languishing in the iron-barred Marshalsea.

As Laurence Sterne has truly said, "Matter grows under one's hands. Let no man say, 'Come, I'll write a duodecimo.'" And so with such a swift-flowing itinerary as would follow the course of a

THE "POOL OF LONDON."
St. Paul's Cathedral in the Distance.

river, it is difficult to get, within a reasonably small compass, any full résumé of the bordering topography of the Thames. All is reminiscent, in one way or another, of any phase of London life in any era, and so having proceeded thus far on the voyage without foundering, one cannot but drop down with the tide, and so to open sea.

Below the metropolis of docks and moorings the river widens to meet the sea, so that any journey of observation must perforce be made upon its bosom rather than as a ramble along its banks.

Blackwall, with its iron-works; Woolwich, with its arsenal; and Greenwich, with its hospital and observatory, are all landmarks by which the traveller to London, by sea, takes his reckoning of *terra firma.*

The shipping of the Orient, the Baltic, the Continent, or the mere coaster, with that unique species of floating thing, the Thames barge, all combine in an apparently inextricable tangle which only opens out in the estuary below Gravesend, which, with its departed glory and general air of decay, is the real casting-off point of seagoing craft. Here the "mud-pilot," as the river pilot is locally known, is dropped, and the "channel pilot" takes charge, and here last leave-takings are said and last messages left behind.

Opposite Gravesend, from where Dickens first set sail for America, is Tilbury Fort, a reminder of the glories of England's arms in the days of Elizabeth. It may be said to be the real outpost of London. Here passing from the " Lower Hope " into " Sea Reach," we fairly enter upon the estuary of the Thames. Here the river has rapidly expanded into an arm of the sea, having widened from two hundred and ninety yards at London Bridge to perhaps four and a half miles at the " London Stone " by Yantlet Creek, where the jurisdiction of the Corporation of London ends.

To the north the Essex shore trends rapidly away toward Yarmouth ; to the south straight to the eastern end of the English Channel, past the historic Medway, with Gad's Hill Place and Higham.

Beyond is Strood, Rochester, Chatham, Maidstone, Canterbury, and Broadstairs, and with the latter place one takes leave, as it were, of England, Dickens, and his personal and literary associations therewith.

"THE GOOSE CLUB."

From a drawing by "Phiz."

MANNERS AND CUSTOMS

*L*ONDON is not a single city, but rather a sequence or confederation of cities. In its multifarious districts there is not only a division of labour, but a classification of society — grade rising above grade, separate yet blended — " a mighty maze, but not without a plan." Says one of her most able and observing historians, " were we not accustomed to the admirable order that prevails, we should wonder how it was preserved." The regular supply of the various food markets alone is a truly wonderful operation, including all the necessaries and, what the Londoner himself supposes to be, all the luxuries of life. The method of distribution is truly astonishing, and only becomes less so to the liver in the midst of it all by reason of his varying degree of familiarity therewith. As to the means of sustenance, no less than livelihood, of a great mass of its population, that is equally a mystery. All among the lower classes are not Fagins nor yet Micawbers. How do the poor live who rise in the morning without a penny in their pockets? How do they manage to sell their labour before they can earn the means of appeasing hunger? What are the contrivances on which they hit to carry on their humble traffic? These and similar questions are those which the economist and the city fathers not only have been obliged to heed, but have got still greater concern awaiting them ahead. Poverty and its allied crime, not necessarily brutalized inherent criminal instinct, but crime nevertheless, are the questions which have got to be met broadly, boldly, and on the most liberal lines by those who are responsible for London's welfare.

During the first half of the nineteenth century the economists will tell one that England's commercial industries stagnated, but perhaps the prodigious leaps which it was taking in the new competitive forces of the new world made this theory into a condition.

In general, however, the tastes of the people were improving, and with the freedom of the newspaper press, and the spread of general literature, there came a desire for many elegancies and refinements hitherto disregarded.

The foundation of the British Museum in 1750, by the purchase of the library and collection of Sir

Hans Sloane, and Montagu House, gave an early
impetus to the movement, which was again furthered
when, in 1801, George III. presented a collection of
Egyptian antiquities, and in 1805 and 1806 were
purchased the Townley and Elgin marbles respec-
tively. The Museum continued to increase until,
in 1823, when George IV. presented his father's
library of sixty-five thousand volumes, Montagu
House was found to be quite inadequate for
its purpose, and the present building, designed
by Sir Robert Smirke, and completed in 1827, was
erected on its site. In making this gift, the king
said, " for the purpose of advancing the literature
of his country, and as a just tribute to the memory
of a parent whose life was adorned with every
public and private virtue."

The magnificent reading-room was not constructed until 1855-57, but it became a " felt want "
from the time when George IV. made his valuable
presentation to the Museum. The great " reading
age " was then only in its infancy.

Early in 1830 George IV. fell ill, and on the 25th
of June he died. During his regency, although he
himself had little to do with the matter, his name
was associated with many splendid triumphs, by
the marvellous progress of intellect, and by remarkable improvements in the liberal arts. With fine

abilities and charming manners. England might have been proud of such a king, but he squandered his talents for his own gratification; alienated himself from all right-minded men; lived a disgraceful life, and died the subject of almost universal contempt. His epitaph has been written thus: "He was a bad son, a bad husband, a bad father, a bad subject, a bad monarch, and a bad friend."

The memory of old London is in no way kept more lively than by the numerous City Companies or Guilds. Established with a good purpose, they rendered useful enough service in their day, but within the last half-century their power and influence has waned, until to-day but three, of the eighty or more, are actually considered as Trading Companies, — the Goldsmiths', the Apothecaries' and the Stationers'.

The first companies, or fraternities, of Anglo-Saxon times gradually evolved themselves into the positive forms in which they have endured till to-day. Just when this evolution came about is obscure. An extinct "Knighten Guild" was licensed by Edgar, a reminiscence of which is supposed to exist to-day in Nightingale Lane, where the Guild was known to have been located.

The oldest of the City Companies now existing is the Weavers' Company, having received its charter from Henry II. Though licensed, these trade organizations were not incorporated until the reign of Edward III., who generously enrolled himself as a member of the Merchant Tailors.

At this time it was ordained that all artificers should choose their trade, and, having chosen it, should practise no other; hence it was that these " Guilds " grew to such a position of wealth and influence, the ancient prototype, doubtless, of the modern " labour unions."

The twelve great City Companies, whose governors ride about in the lord mayor's procession of the 9th of November of each year, are, in order of precedence, ranked as follows: Mercers, Grocers, Drapers, Fishmongers, Goldsmiths, Skinners, Merchant Tailors, Haberdashers, Salters, Ironmongers, Vintners, Cloth-workers.

Allied with these are eighty odd other companies divided into three classes:

I. Those exercising a control over their trades: Goldsmiths, Apothecaries.

II. Those exercising the right of search or marking of wares: the Stationers, at whose " hall " must be entered all books for copyright; the Gunmakers, who " prove " all London-made guns; Saddlers, Pewterers, and Plumbers.

III. Companies into which persons carrying on

certain occupations are compelled to enter: Apothecaries, Brewers, Builders, etc.

The "halls," as they are called, are for the most part extensive quadrangular buildings with a courtyard in the centre.

The most pretentious, from an architectural point of view, are Goldsmiths' Hall in Foster Lane, and Ironmongers' Hall in Fenchurch Street.

Fishmongers' Hall, at the northwest angle of London Bridge, built in 1831, is a handsome structure after the Greek order, with a fine dining-room. The Merchant Tailors' Hall, in Threadneedle Street, has a wonderful banquet-room, with portraits of most of the Kings of England, since Henry VIII., adorning its walls.

Stationers' Hall will perhaps be of the greatest interest to readers of this book. All who have to do with letters have a certain regard for the mysticism which circles around the words, " Entered at Stationers' Hall."

The Stationers' Company was incorporated in 1557; it exercised a virtual monopoly of printing almanacs under a charter of James I. until 1775, when the judges of the Court of Common Pleas decided that their professed patent of monopoly was worthless, the Crown having no power to grant any such exclusive right. Doubtless many another archaic statute is of a like invalidity did but some protestful person choose to take issue therewith. The number of freemen of the company is about 1,100; that of the livery about 450. Printers were formerly obliged to be apprenticed to a member of the company, and all publications for copyright must be entered at their hall. The register of the works so entered for publication commenced from 1557, and is valuable for the light it throws on many points of literary history. The Copyright Act imposes on the company the additional duty of registering all assignments of copyrights. The charities of the company are numerous. In Dickens' time Almanac Day (November 22d) was a busy day at the hall, but the great interest in this species of astrological superstition has waned, and, generally speaking, this day, like all others, is of great quietude and repose in these noble halls, where bewhiskered functionaries amble slowly through the routine in which blue paper documents with bright orange coloured stamps form the only note of liveliness in the entire *ensemble*.

The Goldsmiths' Company assays all the gold and silver plate manufactured in the metropolis, and stamps it with the " hall-mark," which varies each year, so it is thus possible to tell exactly the year in which any piece of London plate was produced.

The out-of-door amusements of society were at this time, as now, made much of. The turf, cricket, and riding to hounds being those functions which took the Londoner far afield. Nearer at home were the charms of Richmond, with its river, and the Star and Garter, and the Great Regatta at Henley, distinctly an affair of the younger element.

Tea-gardens, once highly popular, had fallen into disrepute so far as "society" was concerned. Bagnigge Wells, Merlin's Cave, the London Spa, Marylebone Gardens, Cromwell's Gardens, Jenny's Whim, were all tea-gardens, with recesses, and avenues, and alcoves for love-making and tea-drinking, where an orchestra discoursed sweet music or an organ served as a substitute. An intelligent foreigner, who had published an account of his impressions of England, remarked: "The English take a great delight in the public gardens, near the metropolis, where they assemble and drink tea together in the open air. The number of these in the capital is amazing, and the order, regularity, neatness, and even elegance of them are truly admirable. They are, however, very rarely frequented by people of fashion; but the middle and lower ranks go there often, and seem much delighted with the music of an organ, which is usually played in an adjoining building."

Vauxhall, the *Arabia Felix* of the youth of the eighteenth and nineteenth centuries, was still a fashionable resort, "a very pandemonium of society immorality," says a historian. This can well be believed if the many stories current concerning "prince, duke, and noble, and much mob besides," are accepted.

> " *Here the 'prentice from Aldgate may ogle a toast!*
> *Here his Worship must elbow the knight of the post!*
> *For the wicket is free to the great and the small; —*
> *Sing* Tantarara — *Vauxhall! Vauxhall!* "

The first authentic notice of Vauxhall Gardens appears in the record of the Duchy of Cornwall in 1615, when for two hundred years, through the changes of successive ages, there was conducted a round of gaiety and abandon unlike any other Anglo-Saxon institution. Open, generally, only during the summer months, the entertainment varied from vocal and instrumental music to acrobats, " burlettas," " promenades," and other attractions of a more intellectual nature, and, it is to be feared, likewise of a lesser as well.

The exhibition usually wound up with a display of fireworks, set off at midnight. From 1830 to 1850 the gardens were at the very height of their later festivity, but during the next decade they finally sank into insignificance, and at last flickered out in favour of the more staid and sad amusements of the later Victorian period.

As for the indoor pleasures of society at this time, there were the theatre, the opera, and the concert-room. Dining at a popular restaurant or a gigantic hotel had not been thought of. There were, to be sure, the " assembly-rooms " and the " supper-rooms," but there were many more establishments which catered to the pleasures of the masculine mind and taste than provided a fare of food and amusement which was acceptable to the feminine palate.

Of the men's clubs, Brookes' and White's had long been established, and, though of the proprietary order, were sufficiently attractive and exclusive to have become very popular and highly successful. The other class were those establishments which fulfil the true spirit and province of a club, — where an association of gentlemen join together in the expense of furnishing accommodation of refreshment and reading and lounging rooms. This was the basis on which the most ambitious clubs were founded; what they have degenerated into, in some instances, would defy even a rash man to attempt to diagnose, though many are still run on the conservative lines which do not open their doors to strangers, even on introduction, as with the famous Athenæum Club.

Other clubs, whose names were already familiar in the London of Dickens' day, were the Carleton, Conservative, Reform, University, and perhaps a score of others. As is well known, Dickens was an inordinate lover of the drama, a patron of the theatre himself, and an amateur actor of no mean capabilities. As early as 1837 he had written an operetta, " The Village Coquettes," which he had dedicated to Harley. It was performed, for the first time, on December 6, 1836, at the St. James' Theatre. A London collector possesses the original " hand-bill," announcing a performance of " Used Up " and " Mr. Nightingale's Diary," at the Philharmonic Hall, Liverpool, in 1852, in which Dickens, Sir John Tenniel, and Mark Lemon took part; also a playbill of the performance of " The Frozen Deep," at the " Gallery of Illustration," on Regent Street, on July 4, 1857, " by Charles Dickens and his amateur company before Queen Victoria and the Royal Family."

The painting (1846) by C. R. Leslie, R. A., of Dickens as Captain Boabdil, in Ben Jonson's play of " Every Man in His Humour," is familiar to all Dickens lovers.

The theatres of London, during the later years of Dickens' life, may be divided into two classes: those which were under "royal patronage," and those more or less independent theatres which, if ever visited by royalty, were favoured with more or less unexpected and infrequent visits.

Of the first class, where the aristocracy, and the royal family as well, were pretty sure to be found at all important performances, the most notable were "Her Majesty's," "The Royal Italian Opera House," "The Theatre Royal, Drury Lane." Of the latter class, the most famous — and who shall not say the most deservedly so — were the "Haymarket Theatre," "The Adelphi," "The Lyceum," and the "St. James' Theatre."

"Her Majesty's Theatre," on the western side of the Haymarket, was the original of the two Italian opera-houses in London; it was built in 1790, on the site of an older theatre, burnt down in 1867, and rebuilt in 1869. The freehold of some of the boxes was sold for as much as £8,000 each. The opera season was generally from March to August; but the main attractions and the largest audiences were found from May to July. The "Royal Italian Opera House" occupied the site of the former Covent Garden Theatre, as it does to-day, and was built in 1858 on the ruins of one destroyed by fire.

The building is very remarkable, both within and without. Italian opera was produced here with a completeness scarcely paralleled in Europe. When not required for Italian operas, the building was often occupied by an " English Opera Company," or occasionally for miscellaneous concerts. The " Floral Hall " adjoins this theatre on the Covent Garden side. " Drury Lane Theatre," the fourth on the same site, was built in 1812; its glories live in the past, for the legitimate drama now alternates there with entertainments of a more spectacular and melodramatic character, and the Christmas pantomimes, that purely indigenous English institution. The " Haymarket Theatre," exactly opposite " Her Majesty's," was built in 1821; under Mr. Buckstone's management, comedy and farce were chiefly performed. The " Adelphi Theatre," in the Strand, near Southampton Street, was rebuilt in 1858, when it had for a quarter of a century been celebrated for melodramas, and for the attractiveness of its comic actors. The " Lyceum Theatre," or " English Opera House," at the corner of Wellington Street, Strand, was built in 1834 as an English opera-house, but its fortunes were fluctuating, and the performances not of a definite kind. This was the house latterly taken over by Sir Henry Irving. The " Princess' Theatre," on the north side of Oxford Street, was built in 1830; after a few years of opera and miscellaneous dramas, it became the scene of Mr. Charles Kean's Shakespearian revivals, and now resembles most of the other theatres. "St. James' Theatre," in King Street, St. James', was built for Braham, the celebrated singer. "The Olympic" was a small house in Wych Street, Drury Lane, now destroyed. "The Strand Theatre" was famous for its burlesque extravaganzas, a form of theatrical amusement which of late has become exceedingly popular. The "New Globe Theatre" (destroyed so late as 1902) and "The Gaiety" (at the stage entrance of which are the old offices of *Good Words,* so frequently made use of by Dickens in the later years of his life), and "The Vaudeville," were given over to musical comedy and farce. "The Adelphi," though newly constructed at that time, was then, as now, the home of melodrama.

Others still recognized as popular and prosperous houses were "The Court Theatre," Sloane Square; "The Royalty," in Soho; "The Queen's," in Longacre; "The Prince of Wales'," in Tottenham Street, formerly the Tottenham Theatre. Robertson's comedies of "Caste," "Our Boys," etc., were favourite pieces there. "Sadler's Wells," "Marylebone Theatre," "The Brittania," at Hoxton, "The Standard," in Shoreditch, and "The Pavilion," in Whitechapel, were all notable for size and popularity, albeit those latterly mentioned were of a cheaper class.

South of the river were " Astley's," an old amphitheatre, " The Surrey Theatre," and " The Victoria."

At this time (1870) it was estimated that four thousand persons were employed in London theatres, supporting twelve thousand persons. The public expenditure thereon was estimated at £350,000 annually.

Of " concert rooms," there were " Exeter Hall," " St. James' Hall," " Hanover Square Rooms," " Floral Hall," connected with the Covent Garden Opera, " Willis' Rooms," and the " Queen's Concert Rooms," connected with " Her Majesty's Theatre."

Here were given the performances of such organizations as " The Sacred Harmonic Society," " The Philharmonic Society," " The Musical Union," and the " Glee and Madrigal Societies," " The Beethoven Society," and others.

" Entertainments," an indefinite and mysterious word, something akin to the *olla podrida* of sunny Spain, abounded.

Usually they were a sort of musical or sketch entertainment, thoroughly innocuous, and, while attaining a certain amount of popularity and presumably success to their projectors, were of a nature only amusing to the completely ennuied or juvenile temperament. Readings by various persons, more or less celebrated, not forgetting the name of Dickens, attracted, properly enough, huge crowds, who were willing to pay high prices to hear a popular author interpret his works. A species of lion-taming, which, if not exactly exciting, is harmless and withal edifying. The last two varieties of entertainment usually took place in the " Egyptian Hall," in Piccadilly, " St. James' Hall," or " The Gallery of Illustration " in Regent Street.

Of miscellaneous amusements, appealing rather more to the middle class than the actual society element, — if one really knows what species of human being actually makes up that vague body, — were such attractions as were offered by " Madame Tussaud's Waxwork Exhibition," which suggests at once to the lover of Dickens Mrs. Jarley's similar establishment, and such industrial exhibitions as took place from time to time, the most important of the period of which this book treats being, of course, the first great International Exhibition, held in Hyde Park in 1851.

Further down the social scale the amusements were a variation only of degree, not of kind.

The lower classes had their coffee-shops and, supposedly, in some degree the gin-palaces, which
however, mostly existed in the picturesque vocab-
ulary of the " smug " reformer.

The tavern, the chop-house, and the dining-room
were variants only of the " assembly-rooms," the
" clubs," and the grand establishments of the upper
circles, and in a way performed the same function,
— provided entertainment for mankind.

As for amusements pure and simple, there was
the " music-hall," which, quoting a mid-Victorian
writer, was a place where held forth a *"species
of musical performance, a singular compound of
poor foreign music, but indifferently executed, and
interspersed with comic songs of a most extravagant kind, to which is added or interpolated
what the performers please .to term 'nigger'
dances, athletic and rope-dancing feats, the whole
accompanied by much drinking and smoking."*
Which will pass as a good enough description to
apply to certain establishments of this class to-day,
but which, in reality, loses considerable of its force
by reason of its slurring resentment of what was
in a way an invasion of a foreign custom which
might be expected. sooner or later, to crowd out the
conventional and sad amusements which in the
main held forth, and which in a measure has since

taken place. The only bearing that the matter has to the subject of this book is that some large numbers of the great public which, between sunset and its sleeping hours, must perforce be amused in some way, is to-day, as in days gone by, none too particular as to what means are taken to accomplish it.

There is a definite species of depravity which is supposed to be peculiarly the attribute of the lower classes. If it exists at all to-day, it probably does lie with the lower classes, but contemporary opinion points to the fact that it was not alone in those days the lower classes who sought enjoyment from the cockpit, the dog fight, the prize ring, or the more ancient bull-baiting. all of which existed to some degree in the early nineteenth century. Truly the influence of the Georges on society, of whatever class, must have ' een cruelly debasing, and it was not to be expected that the early years of Victoria's reign should have been able to eradicate it thoroughly, and though such desires may never be entirely abolished, they are, in the main, not publicly recognized or openly permitted to-day, a fact which is greatly to the credit of the improved taste of the age in which we live.

Formerly it was said that there was but one class of hotels in and near London of which the charges could be stated with any degree of precision. The *old* hotels, both at the West End and in the City, kept no printed tariff, and were not accustomed even to be asked beforehand as to their charges. Most of the visitors were more or less *recommended* by guests who had already sojourned at these establishments, and who could give information as to what *they* had paid. Some of the hotels declined even to receive guests except by previous written application, or by direct introduction, and would rather be without those who would regard the bill with economical scrutiny.

Of these old-fashioned hotels, — barbarous relics of another day, — few are to be found now, and, though existing in reality, are being fast robbed of their *clientièle*, which demand something more in the way of conveniences — with no diminution of comforts — than it were possible to get in the two or three private houses thrown into one, and dubbed by the smugly respectable title of " Private Hotel."

Other establishments did exist, it is true, in Dickens' time : " The Golden Cross " and " Morley's," " Haxell's," and others of such class, from which coaches still ran to near-by towns, and which houses catered principally for the country visitor or the avowed commercially inclined. But aside from these, and the exclusive and presumably extravagant class of smaller houses, represented by such names as " Claridge's," " Fenton's," " Limner's," *et als.*, there was no other accommodation except the " taverns " of masculine propensities of Fleet Street and the City generally.

The great joint stock hotels, such as " The Metropole," " The Savoy," and " The Cecil," did not come into being until well toward the end of Dickens' life, if we except the excellent and convenient railway hotels, such as made their appearance a few years earlier, as " Euston," " King's Cross," and " Victoria." The first of the really great modern *caravanserais* are best represented by those now somewhat out-of-date establishments, the " Westminster Palace," " Inns of Court," " Alexandra," and others of the same ilk, while such as the magnificently appointed group of hotels to be found in the West Strand, Northumberland Avenue, or in Pall Mall were unthought of.

The prevailing customs of an era, with respect to clubs, taverns, coffee-houses, etc., mark signally the spirit of the age. The taverns of London, properly so called, were, in the earliest days of their prime, distinguished, each, for its particular class of visitors. The wits and poets met at " Will's " in Covent Garden, and the politicians at " St. James' Coffee-House," from which Steele often dated his *Tatler*. Later, in the forties, there were perhaps five hundred houses of entertainment, as distinguished from the ordinary "public house," or the more ambitious hotel.

The "dining-rooms," "à la mode beef shops," and "chop-houses" abounded in the "City," and with unvarying monotony served four, six, or nine-penny "plates" with astonishing rapidity, quite rivalling in a way the modern "quick lunch." The waiter was usually servile, and in such places as the "Cheshire Cheese," "Simpson's," and "Thomas'," was and is still active. He was a species of humanity chiefly distinguished for a cryptogrammatic system of reckoning your account, and the possessor of as choice a crop of beneath-the-chin whiskers as ever graced a Galway or a County Antrim squireen.

The London City waiter, as distinguished from his brethren of the West End, who are most Teutonic, is a unique character. Here is Leigh Hunt's picture of one:

"He has no feeling of noise; even a loaf with him is hardly a loaf; it is so many 'breads.' His longest speech is making out a bill *viva voce*, — 'Two beefs, one potato, three ales, two wines, six and two pence.'"

A unique institution existed during the first quarter of the last century. Some of Dickens' characters, if not Dickens himself, must have known something of the sort. Charles Knight tells of more than one establishment in the vicinity of the " Royal Exchange," where a sort of public *gridiron* was kept always at hand, for broiling a chop or steak which had been bought by the customer himself at a neighbouring butcher's. For this service, the small sum of a penny was charged, the profit to the house probably arising from the sale of potable refreshments.

The houses which were famous for "fine old cheese," "baked potatoes," "mutton or pork pies," "sheep's trotters," or "pig's faces," were mostly found, or, at least, were at their best, in the "City," though they formed an humble and non-fastidious method of purveying to the demands of hunger, in that the establishments catered, more particularly, to the economically inclined, or even the poorer element of city workers.

The rise from these City eating-houses to the more ambitiously expensive caterers of the "West End" was gradual. Prices and the appointments increased as one journeyed westward through Fleet Street, the Strand, to Piccadilly and Regent Street.

Another institution peculiar to London, in its plan and scope at least, was the "coffee-house" of

1840, evolved from those of an earlier generation, but performing, in a way, similar functions.

At this time a "House of Commons Committee of Inquiry into the Operation of Import Duties" — as was its stupendous title — elicited some remarkable facts concerning the fast increasing number of "coffee-houses," which had grown from ten or twelve to eighteen hundred in twenty-five years. One Pamphilon, who appears to have been the most successful, catering to five hundred or more persons per day, gave evidence to the effect that his house was frequented mostly by "lawyers, clerks, and commercial men, some of them managing clerks, many solicitors, and highly respectable gentlemen, who take coffee in the middle of the day in preference to a more stimulating drink. . . . at the present moment, besides a great number of newspapers every day, I am compelled to take in an increasing number of high-class periodicals. . . . *I find there is an increasing demand for a better class of reading.*"

And thus we see, at that day, even as before and since, a very intimate relation between good living and good reading. The practical person, the wary pedant, and the supercritical will scoff at this, but let it stand.

The "cigar divans" and "chess rooms" were

modifications, in a way, of the "coffee-house," though serving mainly evening refreshment, coffee and a "fine Havana" being ample for the needs of him who would ponder three or four hours over a game of chess.

Of the stilly night, there was another class of peripatetic caterers, the "sandwich man," the "baked 'tato man," the old women who served "hot coffee" to coachmen, and the more ambitious "coffee-stall," which must have been the progenitor of the "Owl Lunch" wagons of the United States.

The baked potato man was of Victorian growth, and speedily became a recognized and popular functionary of his kind. His apparatus was not cumbrous, and was gaudy with brightly polished copper, and a headlight that flared like that of a modern locomotive. He sprang into being somewhere in the neighbourhood of St. George's Fields, near "Guy's," Lant Street, and Marshalsea of Dickenesque renown, and soon spread his operations to every part of London.

The food supply of London and such social and economic problems as arise out of it are usually ignored by the mere guide-book, and, like enough, it will be assumed by many to have little to do with the purport of a volume such as the present. As a matter of fact, in one way or another, it has a great deal to do with the life of the day, using the word in its broadest sense.

England, as is well recognized by all, is wholly subservient to the conditions of trade, so far as edible commodities are concerned, throughout the world. Its beef, its corn, and its flour mainly come from America. Its teas, coffees, and spices mostly from other foreign nations, until latterly, when India and Ceylon have come to the fore with regard to the first named of these. Its mutton from New Zealand or Australia, and even potatoes from France, butter and eggs from Denmark and Brittany, until one is inclined to wonder what species of food product is really indigenous to Britain. At any rate, London is a vast *caravanserai* which has daily to be fed and clothed with supplies brought from the outer world.

In spite of the world-wide fame of the great markets of "Covent Garden," "Smithfield," and "Billingsgate," London is wofully deficient in those intermediaries between the wholesaler and the consumer, the public market, as it exists in most Continental cities and in America.

An article in the *Quarterly Review*, in Dickens' day, — and it may be inferred things have only changed to a degree since that time, — illustrate l. in a whimsical way, the vastness of the supply system. The following is described as the supply of meat, poultry, bread, and beer, for one year: 72 miles of oxen, 10 abreast; 120 miles of sheep, do.; 7 miles of calves, do.; 9 miles of pigs, do.; 50 acres of poultry, close together; 20 miles of hares and rabbits, 100 abreast; a pyramid of loaves of bread, 600 feet square, and thrice the height of St. Paul's; 1,000 columns of hogsheads of beer, each 1 mile high. In mere bulk this perhaps does not convey the impression of large figures, but it is certainly very expressive to imagine, for instance, that one has to eat his way through 72 miles of oxen.

The *water* used in the metropolis was chiefly supplied by the Thames, and by an artificial channel called the New River, which entered on the north side of the metropolis. The water is naturally good and soft. The spots at which it is raised from the Thames used to be within the bounds of the metropolis, at no great distance from the mouths of common sewers; but it is now obtained from parts of the river much higher up, and undergoes a very extensive filtration, with which eight companies are concerned. The returns of the registrar-general showed that the average daily supply of water for all purposes to the London population, during August, 1870, was 127,649,728 gallons, of which it is estimated the supply for domestic purposes

amounted to about 90,000,000 gallons. The total
number of houses fed was 512,540. The metropolis
draws its *coal* supplies principally from the neighbourhood of Newcastle, but largely also from certain inland counties, the import from the latter being
by railway. Newcastle coal is preferred. It arrives in vessels devoted exclusively to the trade;
and so many and so excessive are the duties and
profits affecting the article, that a ton of coal, which
can be purchased at Newcastle for 6s. or 7s., costs,
to a consumer in London, from 28s. to 33s. The
quantity of coal brought to London annually much
exceeds 6,000,000 tons, of which considerably more
than 2,000,000 come by railway.

As for the markets themselves, " Billingsgate,"
the great *depot* for the distribution of fish, is described in that section devoted to the Thames.

" Smithfield," is the great wholesale cattle market,
while " Leadenhall " Market, in the very heart of
the business world of London, is headquarters for
poultry.

A detailed description of " Covent Garden
Market," which deals with vegetables, fruits, and
flowers only, must here suffice.

Covent Garden Market occupies a site which is
exceedingly central to the metropolis. It was once
the garden to the abbey and convent of Westmin-

ster: hence the name *Convent* or *Covent*. At the suppression of the religious houses in Henry VIII.'s reign, it devolved to the Crown. Edward VI. gave it to the Duke of Somerset; on his attainder it was granted to the Earl of Bedford, and in the Russell family it has since remained. From a design of Inigo Jones, who built the banqueting-room at Whitehall, the York Water Gate, and other architectural glories of London, it was intended to have surrounded it with a colonnade; but the north and a part of the east sides only were completed. The fruit and vegetable markets were rebuilt in 1829-30. The west side is occupied by the parish church of St. Paul's, noticeable for its massive roof and portico. Butler, author of "Hudibras," lies in its graveyard, without a stone to mark the spot. In 1721, however, a cenotaph was erected in his honour in Westminster Abbey. The election of members to serve in Parliament for the city of Westminster was formerly held in front of this church, the hustings for receiving the votes being temporary buildings. The south side is occupied by a row of brick dwellings. Within this square thus enclosed the finest fruit and vegetables from home and foreign growers are exposed for sale, cabbages and carrots from Essex and Surrey, tomatoes and asparagus from France and Spain, oranges from Se-

ville and Jaffa, pines from Singapore, and bananas
from the West Indies, not forgetting the humble ,
but necessary potato from Jersey, Guernsey, or
Brittany. A large paved space surrounding the
interior square is occupied by the market-gardeners,
who, as early as four or five in the morning, have
carted the produce of their grounds, and wait to
dispose of it to dealers in fruit and vegetables re-
siding in different parts of London; any remainder
is sold to persons who have standings in the market.
Within this paved space rows of shops are con-
veniently arranged for the display of the choicest
fruits of the season: the productions of the forcing-
house, and the results of horticultural skill, appear
in all their beauty. There are also conservatories,
in which every beauty of the flower-garden may be
obtained, from the rare exotic to the simplest native
flower. The Floral Hall, close to Covent Garden
Opera House, has an entrance from the northeast
corner of the market, to which it is a sort of appendage, and to the theatre. Balls, concerts, etc.,
are occasionally given here. The Farringdon, Borough, Portman, Spitalfields, and other vegetable
markets, are small imitations of that at Covent
Garden.

The greater part of the *corn*, meaning, in this case,
wheat, as well as maize, as Indian corn is known

throughout Great Britain, used for bread and other purposes in the metropolis, is sold by corn-factors at the Corn Exchange, Mark Lane; but the corn itself is not taken to that place. Enormous quantities of flour are also brought in, having been ground at mills in the country and in foreign parts.

The *beer* and *ale* consumed in the metropolis is, of course, vast in quantity, beyond comprehension to the layman. If one could obtain admission to one of the long-standing establishments of Messrs. Barclay & Perkins or Truman & Hanbury, whose names are more than familiar to all who travel London streets, he would there see vessels and operations astonishing for their magnitude — bins that are filled with 2,000 quarters of malt every week; brewing-rooms nearly as large as Westminster Hall; fermenting vessels holding 1,500 barrels each; a beer-tank large enough to float an up-river steamer; vats containing 100,000 gallons each; and 60,000 casks.

PAST AND PRESENT

*T*HE American is keenly alive to all the natural and added beauties of English life, and even more so of London. He does not like to have his ideals dispelled, or to find that some shrine at which he would worship has disappeared for ever, like some " solemn vision and bright silver dream," as becomes a minstrel. For him are the traditions and associations, the sights and sounds, which, as he justly says, have no meaning or no existence for the " fashionable lounger " and the " casual passenger." " The Barbican does not to every one summon the austere memory of Milton; nor Holborn raise the melancholy shade of Chatterton; nor Tower Hill arouse the gloomy ghost of Otway; nor Hampstead lure forth the sunny figure of Steele and the passionate face of Keats; nor old Northumberland Street suggest the burly presence of ' rare Ben Jonson;' nor opulent Kensington revive the stately head of Addison; nor a certain window in Wellington Street reveal in fancy's picture the rugged lineaments and splendid eyes of Dickens." But to the true pilgrim London speaks like the diapason of a great organ. "He stands amid achievements that are finished, careers that are consummated, great deeds that are done, great memories that are immortal; he views and comprehends the sum of all that is possible to human thought, passion, and labour, and then — high over mighty London, above the dome of St. Paul's Cathedral, piercing the clouds, greeting the sun, drawing unto itself all the tremendous life of the great city and all the meaning of its past and present — the golden cross of Christ."

The regular old-fashioned coaches of London were from the first to third quarters of the nineteenth century supplanted by the ark-like omnibus, which even till to-day rumbles roughly through London streets. Most of the places within twenty miles of the metropolis, on every side, were thus supplied with the new means of transportation. The first omnibus was started by Mr. Shillibeer, from Paddington to the Bank, July 4, 1829. From this time to 28th June, 1870, — the number of such vehicles licensed in the Metropolitan District was 1,218. Every omnibus and hackney-carriage within the Metropolitan District and the City of London, and the liberties thereof, has to take out a yearly license, in full force for one year, unless revoked or suspended; and all such licenses are to be granted by the Commissioners of Police, whose officers are constantly inspecting these public vehicles. Generally speaking, each omnibus travels over the same route, and exactly the same number of times, day after day, with the exception of some few of the omnibuses which go longer journeys than the rest, and run not quite so often in winter as in summer.' Hence the former class of omnibus comes to be associated with a particular route. It is known to the passengers by its colour, the name of its owner, the name given to the omnibus itself, or the places to and from which it runs, according to circumstances. The greater portion are now the property of the London General Omnibus Company. The designations given to the omnibuses are generally given on the front in large letters.

At least so it is written in the guide-book. As a matter of fact, the stranger will be fortunate if he can figure out their destination from the mass of hoardings announcing the respective virtues of Venus Soap and Nestlés' Milk. To the Londoner this is probably obvious, in which case the virtues of this specific form of advertising might be expected to be considerably curtailed.

One who was curious of inspecting contrasting

elements might have done worse than to take an outside "garden seat" on a Stratford and Bow omnibus, at Oxford Circus, and riding — for sixpence all the way — *via* Regent Street, Pall Mall, Trafalgar Square, Strand, Fleet Street, St. Paul's, past the Mansion House and the Bank, Royal Exchange, Cornhill, Leadenhall Street, Aldgate, Whitechapel Road, Mile End, to Stratford.

The convenient, if ungraceful, cab had completely superseded the old pair-horse hackney-coaches in London in general use previous to 1850. According to the returns of the day, there were 6,793 of the modern single-horse hackney-coaches in the metropolis altogether, of two different kinds, "four-wheelers" and "hansoms," which took their name from the patentee. The "four-wheelers" are the more numerous; they have two seats and two doors; they carry four persons, and are entirely enclosed. The "hansoms" have seating capacity for but two, and, though convenient and handy beyond any other wheeled thing until the coming of the automobile, the gondola of London was undeniably dangerous to the occupant, and ugly withal, two strongly mitigating features.

Of the great event of Dickens' day, which took place in London, none was greater or more characteristic of the devotion of the British people to

INTERIOR OF ST. PAUL'S CATHEDRAL DURING THE DUKE OF
WELLINGTON'S FUNERAL.

the memory of a popular hero than the grand military funeral of the Right Honourable Field Marshal Arthur Wellesley, Duke of Wellington (November, 1852). Certainly no military pageant of former times — save, possibly, the second funeral of Napoleon — was so immeasurably of, and for, the people. By this time most of the truly great of England's roll of fame had succumbed, died, and were buried with more or less ostentation or sincere display of emotion, but it remained for Wellington — a popular hero of fifty years' standing — to outrival all others in the love of the people for him and his works. He died at Walmer Castle on the Kent coast.

His body lay there in state, at Chelsea Hospital and in St. Paul's Cathedral, before it was finally laid to rest in the marble sarcophagus which is seen to-day in the same edifice. With Nelson, nay, more than Nelson, he shares the fervid admiration of the Briton for a great warrior.

Disraeli's eulogium in the House of Commons appears to have been the one false note of sincerity in all the pæan that went forth, and even this might perhaps have survived an explanation had Beaconsfield chosen to make one. Certainly racial opposition to this great statesman had a great deal to do with the cheap denunciation which was heaped

upon his head because he had made use of the words
of another eulogist, a Frenchman, upon the death
of one of his own countrymen; "a second-rate
French marshal," the press had called him, one
Marshal de St. Cyr. It was unfortunate that
such a forceful expression as this was given second-hand: "*A great general must not only think,
but think with the rapidity of lightning, to be
able to fulfil the highest duty of a minister of
state, and to descend, if need be, to the humble office
of a commissary and a clerk; must be able, too,
to think with equal vigour, depth, and clearness,
in the cabinet or amidst the noise of bullets. This
is the loftiest exercise and most complete triumph
of human faculties.*"

All this, and much more, is absolutely authenticated as having been uttered by M. Thiers twenty
years before the occasion referred to. It is perhaps true that the great Wellington deserved better
than this second-hand eulogy, and perhaps right
that there should have been resentment, but further
comment thereon must be omitted here, save that
the incident is recorded as one of those events of an
age which may well be included when treating of
their contemporary happenings.

No account of the London of any past era could
ignore mention of those great civic events, occurring

on the 9th November in each year, and locally
known as " Lord Mayor's Day," being the occasion
on which that functionary enters into his term of
office. As a pageant, it is to-day somewhat out
of date, and withal, tawdry, but as a memory of
much splendour in the past, it is supposedly continued as one of those institutions which the Briton
is wont to expect through tradition and custom.
Perhaps the following glowing account of one of
these gorgeous ceremonies, when the water pageant
was still in vogue, written by an unknown journalist, or " pressman," as he is rather enigmatically
called in London, in 1843, will serve to best describe
the annually recurring event of pride and glory to
your real Cockney.

LORD MAYOR'S DAY

" ' Oh ! such a day
So renown'd and victorious,
Sure such a day was never seen —
City so gay,
And Cits so uproarious,
As tho' such sight had never been !

" ' All hail ! November —
Though no *hail* to-day
(At least that we remember),
Hath pav'd the way
His Civic Majesty hath will'd to go,
And swore he'd *go* it 'spite hail, rain, or snow !

He takes to *water* for an *airing*,
Before perhaps he dines with Baring
Or sees the waiter, so alert,
    Place the fav'rite *Patties-on*
The table near him — knave expert
    To make the most of " what is on ! "
By this we mean, what's most in season,
To say no more we have a reason ! '

                                   — *Anon.*

" Since the first mayoralty procession, in the year
1215, probably there have been few finer pageants
than that of Thursday last, when the November sun
even gilded with his beams the somewhat tarnished
splendour of the City state.

" According to annual custom, the new lord mayor
(Alderman Magnay) was sworn into his office of
Chief Magistrate of the City of London, at the
Guildhall.

" Being a member of the Stationers' Company, the
master, wardens, and court of assistants of that
company proceeded to Mansion House, where they
were met by the new lord mayor and his sheriffs.
After a sumptuous *déjeûner à la fourchette*, the
whole of the civic dignitaries proceeded to the
Guildhall.

" The next day the various officials assembled at
the Guildhall, and, the procession being formed, proceeded thence through King Street, Cateaton Street,

Moorgate Street, London Wall, Broad Street, Threadneedle Street, Mansion House Street, Poultry, Cheapside, and Queen Street, to Southwark Bridge, where his lordship embarked at the Floating Pier for Westminster. This somewhat unusual arrangement arose from the new lord mayor being the alderman of Vintry Ward, wherein the bridge is situated, and his lordship being desirous that his constituents should witness the progress of the civic procession. The embarkation was a picturesque affair; the lord mayor's state barge, the watermen in their characteristic costume, and the lord mayor and his party were, in civic phrase, 'taking water.'

"The novelty of the point of embarkation drew clustering crowds upon the bridge and the adjoining river banks. There were the usual waterside rejoicings, as the firing of guns, streaming flags, and hearty cheers; and the water procession had all the festal gaiety with which we have been wont to associate it in the past. The scene was very animating, the river being thickly covered with boats of various descriptions, as well as with no less than seven state barges, filled inside and outside with the livery belonging to the City Companies, and all anxiously awaiting the word of command to proceed onward to Westminster. The sun shone resplendently upon the flags and banners studding the tops of the barges, and the wharfs near the spot all exhibited similar emblems. As the new lord mayor entered the City barge, and was recognized, the air was rent with the most deafening shouts of applause, which his lordship gracefully acknowledged by repeatedly bowing to the assembled thousands. The aquatic procession now left the pier, the City barge being accompanied by the Stationers, Fishmongers, Goldsmiths, Wax Chandlers, and Ironmongers' Companies, in their respective state barges.

"On arrival at Westminster, the lord mayor and civic authorities having landed, they walked in procession to the Court of Exchequer, where a large number of ladies and gentlemen awaited their arrival. Having been introduced to the chief baron by the recorder, who briefly stated the qualifications of Alderman Magnay for his important office of chief magistrate, and the learned baron having eloquently replied, the new lord mayor invited his lordship to the inauguration dinner, and afterward proceeded to the other courts, inviting the judge of each court to the same.

"His lordship and the various officials then reëmbarked in the state barge for Blackfriars Bridge, where the procession was re-formed and joined by the ambassadors, her Majesty's ministers, the nobility, judges, members of Parliament, and various

LORD MAYOR'S PROCESSION, ASCENDING LUDGATE HILL.

other persons of distinction. The whole then moved through Ludgate Hill, St. Paul's Churchyard, Cheapside, and down King Street to the Guildhall, where the inaugural entertainment was to be given.

"The plate given herein shows the return of the procession, just as the gorgeous state coach is about to wend its way up Ludgate Hill. The coach is, doubtless, the most imposing feature of the modern show, and has thus played its part for nearly four-score years and ten. It is a piece of cumbrous magnificence, better assorting with the leisurely progress of other days than the notions of these progressive times. Yet it is a sight which may have inspired many a City apprentice, and spurred him onward to become an 'honourable of the land;' it is, moreover, the very type of this 'red-letter day' in the City; and, costly as it is, with its disappearance, even portly aldermen will vanish into thin air.

"The foremost group shows the lord mayor seated in the coach, attended by his chaplain, and the sword and mace-bearers, the former carrying — which has to be held outside the coach, be it observed; its stature is too great for it to find shelter inside — the pearl sword presented to the City by Queen Elizabeth, upon opening the Royal Exchange; the latter supporting the great gold mace given by Charles I. The coach is attended by the lord mayor's beadles in their gold-laced cloaks, and carrying small maces.

"Onward are seen the other leading features of the procession; the crowd is truly dense, for at this point is the great crush of the day; 'the Hill' is thronged, and the City police require all their good temper to 'keep the line.' The scene is exciting, and the good-humoured crowd presents many grotesque points for those who delight in studies of character. Altogether, the scene is as joyous, if rather gaudy, picture of a civic holiday as the times could present."

Perhaps the greatest topographical change in the London of Dickens' day was the opening, on November 6, 1869, of the Holborn Viaduct. This improvement was nothing short of the actual demolition and reconstruction of a whole district, formerly either squalid, over-blocked, and dilapidated in some parts, or oversteep and dangerous to traffic in others. But a short time before that same Holborn Valley was one of the most heartbreaking impediments to horse traffic in London, with a gradient on one side of one in eighteen, while opposite it was one in twenty. Thus everything on wheels, and every foot-passenger entering the City by the Holborn route, had to descend twenty-six feet to the Valley of the Fleet, and then ascend a like number to Newgate. The new Viaduct levelled all this, and made the journey far easier than that by Ludgate Hill.

The greatest architectural work which took shape in London during Dickens' day was the construction of the new Houses of Parliament. Associated intimately with Dickens' first steps to success were the old buildings, which were burned in 1834. Here he received his first regular journalistic employment, as reporter for the *True Sun*, an event which soon led to the acceptance of his writings elsewhere. Some discussion has recently been rife in London concerning the name of the paper with which Dickens had his first Parliamentary employment.

According to Forster, Dickens was in his twenty-third year when he became a reporter on the *Morning Chronicle*. At this time the *Chronicle* was edited by John Black, who had conducted it ever since Perry's death, and the office of the paper from June, 1834, until it died in 1862, was 332 Strand, opposite Somerset House, a building pulled down under the Strand improvement scheme. It had then been for nearly forty years — ever since the *Chronicle* vacated it, in fact — the office of another newspaper, the *Weekly Times and Echo*. It may be

worth while to add that Dickens first entered " The
Gallery " at the age of nineteen, as reporter for the
True Sun, and that he afterward reported during
two sessions for the *Mirror of Parliament* before
he joined the staff of the *Morning Chronicle*.

The new Houses of Parliament form one of the
grandest administrative piles of any city in the
world, built though, it is feared, of a stone too soon
likely to decay, and with a minuteness of Gothic
ornament which is perhaps somewhat out of keeping with a structure otherwise so massive.

The House of Peers is 97 feet long, 45 wide, and
45 high. It is so profusely painted and gilt, and the
windows are so darkened by deep-tinted stained
glass, that it is with difficulty that the details can
be observed. At the southern end is the gorgeously
gilt and canopied throne; near the centre is the
woolsack, on which the lord chancellor sits; at the
end and sides are galleries for peeresses, reporters,
and strangers; and on the floor of the house are the
cushioned benches for the peers. Two frescoes by
David Maclise — " The Spirit of Justice " and
" The Spirit of Chivalry " — are over the strangers'
gallery, as well as a half-dozen others by famous
hands elsewhere. In niches between the windows
and at the ends are eighteen statues of barons who
signed Magna Charta. The House of Commons,

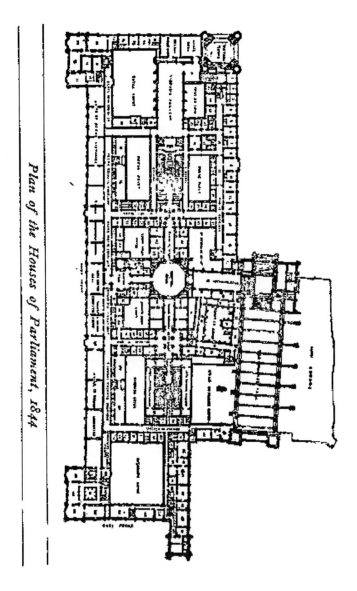

Plan of the Houses of Parliament, 1844

62 feet long, 45 broad, and 45 high, is much less elaborate than the House of Peers. The Speaker's chair is at the north end, and there are galleries along the sides and ends. In a gallery behind the Speaker, the reporters for the newspapers sit. Over which is the ladies' gallery, where the view is ungallantly obstructed by a grating. The present ceiling is many feet below the original one, the room having been to this extent spoiled because the former proportions were bad for hearing.

On the side nearest to Westminster are St. Stephen's Porch, St. Stephen's Corridor, the Chancellor's Corridor, the Victoria Tower, the Royal Staircase, and numerous courts and corridors. At the south end, nearest Millbank, are the Guard Room, the Queen's Robing-Room, the Royal Gallery, the Royal Court, and the Prince's Chamber. The river front is mostly occupied by libraries and committee-rooms. The northern or Bridge Street end displays the Clock Tower and the Speaker's Residence. In the interior of the structure are vast numbers of lobbies, corridors, halls, and courts. The Victoria Tower, at the southwest angle of the entire structure, is a wonderfully fine and massive tower; it is 75 feet square and 340 feet high. The clock tower, at the north end, is 40 feet square and 320 feet high, profusely gilt near the top. After two attempts made to supply this tower with a bell of fourteen tons weight, and after both failed, one of the so-called " Big Bens," the weight of which is about eight tons (the official name being " St. Stephen "), now tells the hour in deep tones. There are, likewise, eight smaller bells to chime the quarters. The clock is by far the largest and finest in England. There are four dials on the four faces of the tower, each 22½ feet in diameter; the hour figures are 2 feet high and 6 feet apart; the minute marks are 14 inches apart; the hands weigh more than 2 cwt. the pair; the minute hand is 16 feet long, and the hour hand 9 feet; the pendulum is 15 feet long and weighs 680 lbs. The central tower rises to a height of 300 feet.

Its rooms and staircases are almost inconceivably numerous. The river front is nine hundred feet in length, with an elaborately decorated façade with carven statues and emblems. By 1860 the cost had exceeded by a considerable sum £2,000,000.

The growth of the British Museum and its ever increasing store of knowledge is treated elsewhere, but it is worth recording here, as one of the significant events of contemporary times, the opening of the present structure with its remarkable domed reading-room.

This great national establishment contains a vast

and constantly increasing collection of books, maps, drawings, prints, sculptures, antiquities, and natural curiosities. It occupies a most extensive suite of buildings in Great Russell Street, Bloomsbury, commenced in 1823, and only finished during the last quarter of the nineteenth century. It has cost a sum little less than £1,000,000. Sir 'chard Smirke was the architect. The principal, or south front, 370 feet long, presents a range of forty-four columns, with a majestic central portico, with a sculptured pediment. Since its commencement, in 1755, the collection has been prodigiously increased by gifts, bequests, and purchases; and now it is, perhaps, the largest of the kind in the world. The library contains more than eight hundred thousand volumes, and is increasing enormously in extent every year. The magnificent reading-room is open only to persons who proceed thither for study. or for consulting authorities. It was opened in 1857, and built at a cost of £150,000, and is one of the finest and most novel apartments in the world; it is circular, 140 feet in diameter, and open to a dome-roof 106 feet high, supported entirely without pillars. This beautiful room, and the fire-proof galleries for books which surround it, were planned by Mr. Panizzi, an Italian and a former keeper of the printed books.

In connection with the library proper is an equally vast collection of antiquities, etc., of which all guide-books and those publications issued by the Museum authorities tell.

The building was complete by 1865, and for the last forty years has stood proudly in its commanding situation, the admiration of all who have come in contact therewith.

What Hampstead Heath is to the coster, the Crystal Palace is to the middle-class Londoner, who repairs there, or did in Dickens' time, on every possible auspicious occasion. This structure itself, though it can hardly be called beautiful by the most charitably disposed, is in many respects one of the most remarkable in the world, and owes its existence to the Great Exhibition of 1851 in Hyde Park. The materials of that building, being sold to a new company toward the close of that year, were transferred to an elevated spot near Sydenham, seven miles from town, to the south. The intention was to found a palace and park for the exhibition of art and science on a paying basis. The original estimate was £500,000, but the expenditure was nearly £1,500,000, too great to assure a probable profitable return.

The palace and grounds were opened in 1854, the towers and fountains some time after.

The building itself is 1,600 feet long and 380 wide, and at the transept is nearly 200 feet in height. Exhibition-rooms, reading-rooms, restaurants, and a vast orchestral auditorium were included under one roof, with bazaars and small shops and stalls innumerable.

The parks and garden were laid out to cover some two hundred acres, with terraces and fountains galore, the idea being to produce somewhat the effect as at Versailles, with Les Grande and Petite Eaux, on "grand days" the fountains consuming over 6,000,000 gallons. Cricket, football, and sports of various kinds used to draw vast throngs to "the Palace," and the firework displays at night were, and are to-day, justly celebrated. In short, this "Cockney Arcadia," if rather a tawdry attraction, has had the benefit of much honest admiration of the Londoner, who perforce could not get farther afield for his holiday, and its like can hardly be said to exist elsewhere in Europe or America. Hence it must perforce rank in a way as something unique in present-day outdoor entertainment, as near as is left to us of those of the days of Ranelegh and Vauxhall. Beloved of the clerk and shopkeeper, and altogether an attraction which few of their class appear to be able to resist for long at a time.

London is no more the dread of the visitor who

feared the ways that are dark and the tricks that
are vain.

London tricks are old as London's history, and
from the days of Chaucer the countryman's fear of
London's vastness and the cheats practised by her
nimble-witted rogues have passed into literature.
In the year 1450 John Lydgate sang the sorrows of
a simple Kentish wight, who found that, go where
he would in London, he could not speed without
money:

> "To London once, my stepps I bent,
> Where trouth in no wyse shoulf be faynt;
> To Westmynster ward I forthwith went,
> To a man of law to make complaynt.
> I sayd, 'for Mary's love, that holy saynt!
> Pity the poor that would proceede;'
> But for lack of mony I cold not spede."

After going among the lawyers of King's Bench,
the Flemings of Westminster Hall with their hats
and spectacles, the cloth men and drapers of Cheapside, and the butchers of Eastcheap, poor Lackpenny
found that nowhere, without money, could he be
sped in London. His final adventure and reflections
were these:

> "Then hyed I me to Belynsgate;
> And one cryed 'hoo, go we hence!'
> I prayd a barge man for God's sake,
> That he wold spare me my expence.

'Thou scapst not here,' quod he, 'under 2 pence,
I lyst not yet bestow my almes dede;'
Thus lacking mony I could not spede.

"Then I convayed me into Kent;
For of the law wold I meddle no more
Because no man to me tooke entent,
I dyght me to do as I dyd before.
Now Jesus that in Bethlem was bore,
Save London, and send trew lawyers there mede,
For who so wants mony with them shall not spede."

Again one might quote that old Roxburghe ballad,
"The Great Boobee," in which a country yokel is
made to tell how he was made to look foolish when
he resolved to plough no more, but to see the fashions of London:

"Now as I went along the street,
I carried my hat in my hand,
And to every one that I did meet
I bravely bent my band.
Some did laugh, some did scoff,
And some did mock at me,
And some did say I was a woodcock,
And a great Boobee.

"Then I did walk in haste to Paul's,
The steeple for to view,
Because I heard some people say
't should be builded new.
When I got up unto the top,
The city for to see,
It was so high, it made me cry,
Like a great Boobee.

. . . .
" Next day I thorugh Pye-corner past,
The roast meat on the stall
Invited me to take a taste ;
My money was but small :
The meat I pickt, the cook me kickt,
As 1 may tell to thee,
He beat me sore, and made me rore,
Like a great Boobee."

It should be remembered, however, that the great
classic of London every-day life, Gay's " Trivia,"
with its warnings against every danger of the street,
from chairmen's poles to thimblerigging, from the
ingenious thefts of periwigs to the nuisances caused
by dustmen and small coalmen, from the reckless
horseplay of the Mohawks to the bewilderment
which may overtake the stranger confronted by the
problem of Seven Dials, was written for the warn-
ing of Londoners themselves. Those were the days
when diamond cut diamond.

In the last fifty years the roving swindler has
become rare in the streets. London now frightens
the countryman more by its size than anything else.
And yet the bigger London grows the more it must
lose even this power to intimidate. Its greatest distances, its vast suburban wildernesses, are seen by
him only through a railway carriage window. He
is shot into the centre, and in the centre he remains,

where help and convenience are increased every year.
It was different in the old days, when the countryman rolled into London by coach, and was robbed
on Hounslow Heath before he had seen more than
the light of London in the sky. No one nowadays
is in danger of being driven mad by the mere spec-
tacle of London opening out before him, yet this
was the fate of a West Country traveller who saw
London for the first time from a coach early in the
nineteenth century. Cyrus Redding tells the story
in his entertaining " Fifty Years' Recollections."
All went well as far as Brentford. Seeing the lamps
of that outlying village, the countryman imagined
that he was at his journey's end, but as mile after
mile of illumination went on, he asked, in alarm,
" Are we not yet in London, and so many miles of
lamps? "   At last, at Hyde Park Corner, he was
told that this was London; but still on went the
lamps, on and on the streets, until the poor stranger
subsided into a coma of astonishment. When at
last they entered Lad Lane, the great Cheapside
coaching centre, a travelling companion bade the
West Countryman remain in the coffee-room while
he made inquiries. On returning, he found no trace
of him, nor heard any more of him for six weeks.
He then learned that he was in custody at Sher-
borne, in Dorsetshire, as a lunatic. He was taken

home, and after a brief return of his reason he died. He was able to explain that he had become more and more bewildered by the lights and by the never-ending streets, from which he thought he should never be able to escape. Somehow, he walked blindly westward, and at last emerged into the country, only to lose his memory and his wits.

Things are different to-day, and yet many people from the remoter parts of England are bewildered, distressed, and crazed by a visit to London. One meets them drifting wearily and anxiously toward King's Cross or St. Pancras at the end of their stay. They will be happy again when they see the utensils glitter on their old kitchen wall; when they have peeped into their best room and found the shade of stuffed squirrels resting undisturbed on the family Bible; and when the steam rises above their big blue teacups more proudly than ever the dome of St. Paul's soars above this howling Babylon, then they will acquiesce in all that is said in praise of the Abbey, the Bank of England, and Madam Tussaud's.

THE UNDER WORLD

*A*S for the people of Dickens and the people he knew so well, they were mostly of the lower middle classes, though he himself had, by the time his career was well defined, been able to surround himself with the society of the leading literary lights of his time.

Surely, though, the Cockney *pur sang* never had so true a delineator as he who produced those pen-pictures ranging all the way from the vulgarities of a Sykes to the fastidiousness of a Skimpole. It is a question, wide open in the minds of many, as to whether society of any rank is improving or not; surely the world is quite as base as it ever was, and as worthily circumspect too. But while the improvement of the aristocracy in general, since mediæval times, in learning and accomplishments, was having its untold effect on the middle classes, it was long before the immense body of workers, or perhaps one should say skilled labourers, as the economists call them, partook in any degree of the general amendment. Certainly we have a right to assume, even with a twentieth-century standpoint to judge from, that there was a constantly increasing dissemination of knowledge, if not of culture, and that sooner or later it might be expected to have its desired, if unconscious, effect on the lower classes. That discerning, if not discreet, American, Nathaniel Parker Willis, was inclined to think not, and compared the English labourer to a tired donkey with no interest in things about him, and with scarce surplus energy enough to draw one leg after the other. He may have been wrong, but the fact is that there is a very large proportion of Dickens' characters made up of a shiftless, worthless, and even criminal class, as we all recognize, and these none the less than the other more worthy characters are nowhere to be found as a thoroughly indigenous type but in London itself.

There was an unmistakable class in Dickens' time, and there is to-day, whose only recourse, in their moments of ease, is to the public house, — great, strong, burly men, with "a good pair of hands," but no brain, or at least no development of it, and it is to this class that your successful middle-Victorian novelist turned when he wished to suggest something unknown in polite society. This is the individual who cares little for public

improvements, ornamental parks. Omnibuses or
trams, steamboats or flying-machines, it's all the
same to him. He cares not for libraries, reading-
rooms, or literature, cheap or otherwise, nothing,
in fact, which will elevate or inspire self-respect;
nothing but soul-destroying debauchery and vice,
living and dying the life of the beast, and as careless
of the future. This is a type, mark you, gentle
reader, which is not overdrawn, as the writer has
reason to know; it existed in London in the days of
Dickens, and it exists to-day, with the qualification
that many who ought, perforce of their instincts,
to be classed therewith do just enough work of an
incompetent kind to keep them well out from under
the shadow of the law; these are the "Sykeses"
of a former day, not the "Fagins," who are possessed of a certain amount of natural wit, if it be
of a perverted kind.

An event which occurred in 1828, almost unpar-
alleled in the annals of criminal atrocity, is significantly interesting with regard to Dickens' absorp-
tion of local and timely accessory, mostly of fact
as against purely imaginative interpolation merely:

A man named Burke (an Irishman) and a woman
named Helen M'Dougal, coalesced with one Hare
in Edinburgh to murder persons by wholesale, and
dispose of their bodies to the teachers of anatomy.

According to the confession of the principal actor, sixteen persons, some in their sleep, others after intoxication, and several in a state of infirmity from disease, were suffocated. One of the men generally threw himself on the victim to hold him down, while the other "burked" him by forcibly pressing the nostrils and mouth, or the throat, with his hands. Hare being admitted as king's evidence, Burke and his other partner in guilt were arraigned on three counts. Helen M'Dougal was acquitted and Burke was executed.

This crime gave a new word to our language. To "burke" is given in our dictionaries as "to murder by suffocation so as to produce few signs of violence upon the victim." Or to bring it directly home to Dickens, the following quotation will serve:

"'You don't mean to say he was "burked," Sam?' said Mr. Pickwick."

With no class of society did Dickens deal more successfully than with the sordidness of crime. He must have been an observer of the most acute perceptions, and while in many cases it was only minor crimes of which he dealt, the vagaries of his assassins are unequalled in fiction. He was generally satisfied with ordinary methods, as with the case of Lawyer Tulkinghorn's murder in Lincoln's Inn Fields, but even in this scene he does throw into crime something more than the ordinary methods of the English novelist. He had the power, one might almost say the Shakespearian power, of not only describing a crime, but also of making you feel the sensation of crime in the air. First and foremost one must place the murder of Montague Tigg.

The grinning Carker of "Dombey and Son" is ground to death under the wheels of a locomotive at a French railway station; Quilp, of "The Old Curiosity Shop," is dramatically drowned; Bill Sykes' neck is broken by the rope meant for his escape; Bradley Headstone and his enemy go together to the bottom of the canal; while the mysterious Krook, of "Bleak House," is disposed of by spontaneous combustion.

Certainly such a gallery of horrors could not be invented purely out of an imaginative mind, and must admittedly have been the product of intimate first-hand knowledge of criminals and their ways.

Doubtless there was a tendency to improve moral conditions as things went on. Britain is not the dying nation which the calamity howlers would have us infer.

In the year 1800, there were — notwithstanding the comparative sparseness of population — eighteen prisons in London alone, whereas in 1850, when Dickens was in his prime and when population had enormously increased, that number had been reduced one-third.

In the early days the jailor in many prisons received no salary, but made his livelihood from the fees he could extort from the prisoners and their friends; and in some cases he paid for the privilege of holding office. Not only had a prisoner to pay for his food and for the straw on which he slept, but, if he failed to pay, he would be detained until he did so.

In Cold Bath Fields prison, men, women, and children were indiscriminately herded together, without employment or wholesome control; while smoking, gaming, singing, and every species of brutalizing conversation obtained.

At the Fleet Prison there was a grate or iron-barred window facing Farringdon Street, and above it was inscribed, " Pray remember the poor prisoners having no allowance," while a small box was placed on the window-sill to receive the charity of the passers-by. and a man ran to and fro, begging coins " for the poor prisoners in the Fleet."

At Newgate, the women usually numbered from a hundred to one hundred and thirty, and each had only eighteen inches breadth of sleeping-room, and all were "packed like slaves in the hold of a slave-ship."

And Marshalsea, which Dickens incorporated into " David Copperfield " and " Little Dorrit," was quite as sordid, to what extent probably none knew so well as Dickens, *père et fils,* for here it was that the father fretfully served out his sentence for debt.

Of all the prisons of that day it may be stated that they were hotbeds of immorality, where children herded with hoary criminals; where no sanitary laws were recognized; where vermin swarmed and disease held forth, and where robbery, tyranny, and cruelty, if not actually permitted, was at least winked at or ignored.

In 1829 Sir Robert Peel brought into force his new police establishment, an event which had not a little to do with the betterment of social life of the day.

" The whole metropolitan district was formed into five local divisions, each division into eight sections, and each section into eight beats, the limits of all being clearly defined and distinguished by letters and numbers; the force itself was divided into companies, each company having one superintendent, four inspectors, sixteen sergeants, and one hundred and forty-four police constables, being also sub-divided into sixteen parts, each consisting of a sergeant and nine men." Incalculable as the boon was in the repression of crime, the Corporation of the City of London could not be persuaded, until several years afterward, to follow such an example, and give up their vested interests in the old system of watchmen. The police system, as remodelled by Sir Robert Peel in 1829, was, of course, the foundation of the present admirable body of constabulary, of which the London "Bobby" must be admitted by all as ranking at the very head of his contemporaries throughout the civilized world. Certainly no more affable and painstaking servants of the public are anywhere to be found; they are truly the "refuge of the inquiring stranger and timid women."

The London policeman, then, is essentially a product of our own times; a vast advance over the peripatetic watchman of a former day, and quite unlike his brother on the Continent, who has not only to keep the peace, but act as a political spy as well. Perhaps it is for this reason that the London policeman is able to exhibit such devotion and affability in the conduct of his duties. Surely no writer or observer has ever had the temerity to assail the efficiency of the London "Peeler" or "Bobby," as he now exists.

No consideration or estimate of middle-class London would be complete without mention of that very important factor in its commissariat — beer, or its various species, mild or bitter, pale or stale. Your true Cockney East-Ender, however, likes his 'arf and 'arf, and further admonishes the cheery barmaid to " draw it mild." Brewers, it would seem, like their horses and draymen, are of a substantial race; many of the leading brewers of the middle nineteenth-century times, indeed, of our own day, are those who brewed in the reigns of the Georges.

By those who know, genuine London ale (presumably the " Genuine Stunning ale " of the " little public house in Westminster," mentioned in " Copperfield ") alone is supposed to rival the ideal " berry-brown " and " nut-brown " ale of the old songs, or at least what passed for it in those days.

The increase of brewers has kept pace with London's increase in other respects. Twenty-six brewhouses in the age of Elizabeth became fifty-five in the middle of the eighteenth century, and one hundred and forty-eight in 1841; and in quantity from 284,145 barrels in 1782 to 2,119,447 in 1836. To-day, in the absence of any statistics to hand, the sum total must be something beyond the grasp of any but the statistician.

Without attempting to discuss the merits or demerits of temperance in general, or beer in particular, it can be safely said that the brewer's dray is a prominent and picturesque feature of London streets, without which certain names, with which even the stranger soon becomes familiar, would be meaningless; though they are, as it were, on everybody's tongue and on many a sign-board in nearly every thoroughfare. As a historian, who would have made an unexceptionable literary critic, has said: Beer overflows in almost every volume of Fielding and Smollett. Goldsmith was not averse to the "*parson's black champagne;*" Hogarth immortalized its domestic use, and Gilray its political history; and the "pot of porter" and "mug of bitter" will go down in the annals of the literature, art, and history of London, and indeed all Britain, along with the more aristocratic port and champagne.

LONDON TOPOGRAPHY

From Park Land to Wapping, by day and by night,
    I've many a year been a roamer,
And find that no Lawyer can London indite,
    Each street, every Lane's a misnomer.
I find Broad Street, St. Giles, a poor narrow nook,
    Battle Bridge is unconscious of slaughter,
Duke's Place can not muster the ghost of a Duke,
    And Brook Street is wanting in water.
          JAMES SMOTH, *Comic Miscellanies.*

*I*T is not easy to delimit the territorial confines of a great and growing city like London. The most that the most sanguine writer could hope to do would be to devote himself to recounting the facts and features, with more or less completeness, of an era, or an epoch, if the word be thought to confine the period of time more definitely.

There is no London of to-day: like "unborn to-morrow" and "dead yesterday," it does not exist. Some remains there may be of a former condition, and signs there assuredly are of still greater things to come, but the very face of the earth in the great world of London is constantly changing and being

Billingsgate and the Custom
House.

The Bank, Royal Exchange,
and Mansion House.

General Post - Office.

King William Street and
Gracechurch Street.

St. Paul's, Cheapside, and
Paternoster Row.

Fleet Street at Temple Bar.

"The City" — London.

improved or disimproved, accordingly as its makers
have acted wisely or not.

The London of Dickens' time — the middle Victorian period — was undergoing, in some degree,
at least, the rapid changes which were making themselves felt throughout the civilized world. New
streets were being put through, old landmarks were
being removed, and new and greater ones rising in
their stead; roadways were being levelled, and hills
were disappearing where they were previously
known. How curious it is that this one topographical detail effects so great a change in the aspect
of the buildings which border upon the streets.
Take for instance the Strand as it exists to-day.
Dickens might have to think twice before he would
know which way to turn to reach the *Good Words*
offices. This former narrow thoroughfare has been
straightened, widened, and graded until about the
only recognizable feature of a quarter of a century
ago is the sky-line. Again, St. Martin's-in-the-
Fields, a noble and imposing church, is manifestly
made insignificant by the cutting down of the grade,
and even removing the broad and gentle rising flight
of steps which once graced its façade. Generally
speaking, the reverse is the case, the level of the
roadway being immeasurably raised, so that one
actually steps down into a building which formerly

was elevated a few steps. All this and much more is a condition which has worked a wondrous change in the topography of London, and doubtless many another great city.

As for grandeur and splendour, that can hardly be claimed for any city which does not make use of the natural features to heighten the effect of the embellishments which the hand of man has added to what nature has already given. London possesses these features to a remarkable degree, and she should make the best of them, even if to go so far as to form one of those twentieth-century innovations, known as an " Art Commission," which she lacks. Such an institution might cause an occasional " deadlock," but it would save a vast deal of disfigurement; for London, be it said, has no streets to rank among those of the world which are truly great, such as High Street at Oxford, and Princess Street in Edinburgh, to confine the comparison to Great Britain.

The author of this book has never had the least thought of projecting " a new work on London," as the industrious author or compiler of Knight's " Old and New London " put it in 1843, when he undertook to produce a monumental work which he declared should be neither a " survey nor a history." The fact is, however, that not even the most sanguine of those writers who may hope to say a new word about any subject so vast as that comprehended by the single word, London, could even in a small measure feel sure that he has actually discovered any new or hitherto unknown fact. In short, one may say that this would be impossible.

London's written history is very extensive and complete, and it is reasonable to suppose that most everything of moment has at one time or another been written down, but there are constantly varying conditions and aspects which do present an occasional new view of things, even if it be taken from an old standpoint; hence even within the limits of which this section treats it is possible to give something of an impression which once and again may strike even a supercritical reader as being timely and pertinent, at least to the purport of the volume.

The latter-day City and County of London, including the metropolitan and suburban area, literally "Greater London," has within the last few years grown to huge proportions. From being a city hemmed within a wall, London has expanded in all directions, gradually forming a connection with various clusters of dwellings in the neighbourhood. It has, in fact, absorbed towns and villages to a considerable distance around: the chief of these

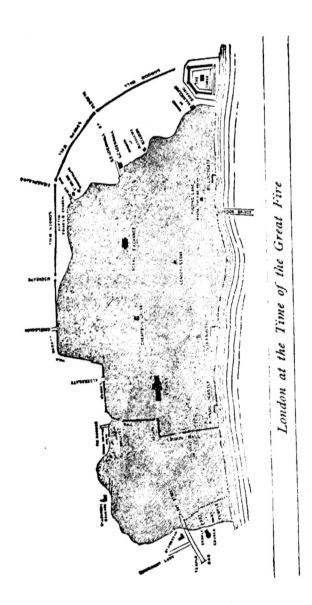

London at the Time of the Great Fire

once detached seats of population being the city of Westminster. By means of its bridges, it has also absorbed Southwark, Bermondsey, Lambeth, and Vauxhall, besides many hamlets and villages beyond.

Even in Dickens' day each centre of urban life, whether it be Chelsea, Whitechapel, or the Borough, — that ill-defined centre south of London Bridge, — was closely identified with local conditions which were no part of the life of any other section. Aside from the varying conditions of social life, or whether the section was purely residential, or whether it was a manufacturing community, there were other conditions as markedly different. Theatres, shops, and even churches varied as to their method of conduct, and, in some measure, of their functions as well. It was but natural that the demand of the Ratcliffe Highway for the succulent "kipper" should conduce to a vastly different method of purveying the edible necessities of life from that of the West End poulterer who sold only Surrey fowl, or, curiously enough, as he really does, Scotch salmon. So, too, with the theatres and music-halls; the lower riverside population demand, if not necessarily a short shrift, a cheap fare, and so he gets his two and three performances a night at a price ranging from three pence to two shillings for what in the west brings from one to ten shillings.

To vary the simile still farther, but without going into the intricacies of dogma, the church has of necessity to appeal to its constituency in the slums in a vastly different method of procedure from what would be considered dignified or even devout elsewhere; and it is a question if the former is not more efficacious than the latter. And so these various centres, as they may be best described, are each of themselves local communities welded, let us hope, into as near as may be a perfect whole, with a certain leeway of self-government and privilege to deal with local conditions.

In 1850, taken as best representative of Dickens' time, London was divided into twenty-six wards (and several liberties). The "Out Parishes" of the "City," the City of Westminster, and the five "Parliamentary Boroughs" of Marylebone, Lambeth, Southwark, Finsbury, and Tower hamlets, and a region of debatable land lying somewhere between that which is properly called London and its environs, and partaking in a certain measure of the attributes of both.

London would seem to be particularly fortunate in its situation, and that a large city should have grown up here was perhaps unavoidable: suffi-

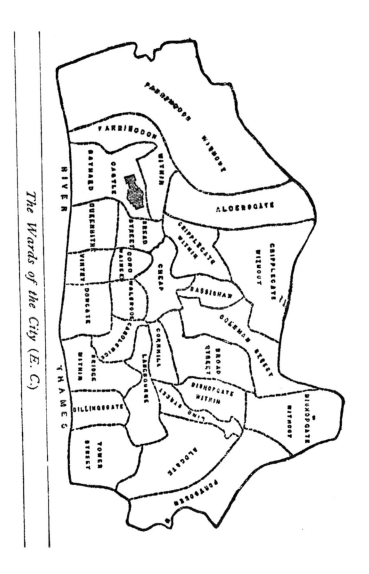

The Wards of the City (E. C.)

ciently far from the open sea to be well protected therefrom, yet sufficiently near thereto to have early become a powerful city and a great port.

Roman occupation, in spite of historians to the contrary, has with the later Norman leavened the Teutonic characteristics of the people of Britain perhaps more than is commonly credited. Cæsar's invasion was something more than a mere excursion, and his influence, at least afterward, developed the possibilities of the " mere collection of huts " with the Celtic name into the more magnificent city of Londinium.

It has been doubted if Cæsar really did know the London of the Britons, which historians have so assiduously tried to make a great and glorious city even before his time. More likely it was nothing of the sort, but was simply a hamlet, set down in a more or less likely spot, around which naturally gathered a slowly increasing population.

In a way, like the Celtic hill towns of Normandy and Brittany, it took Roman impulse to develop it into anything more beautiful and influential than the mere stockade or *zareba* of the aborigine. The first mention of London is supposed to be in the works of Tacitus, a century and a half after Cæsar's invasion. From this it would appear that by the year 62, in the reign of Nero, *Londinium* was already a place of "great importance."

Against the Roman domination the Britons finally rose at the call of the outraged Boadicea, who marched directly upon London as the chief centre of power and civilization. Though why the latter condition should have been resented it is still difficult to understand. Ptolemy, who, however, got much of his information second-hand, refers to London in his geography of the second century as *Londinion*, and locates it as being situate somewhere south of the Thames. All this is fully recounted in the books of reference, and is only mentioned as having more than a little to do with the modern city of London, which has grown up since the great fire in 1666.

As a British town it occupied a site probably co-extensive only with the later Billingsgate and the Tower on one hand, and Dowgate on the other. Lombard and Fenchurch Streets were its northerly limits, with the Wall-Brook and Sher-Bourne on the west. These limits, somewhat extended, formed the outlines of the Roman wall of the time of Theodosius (394).

Coming to a considerably later day, a matter of twelve hundred years or so, it is recalled that the period of the great fire is the time from which the building up of the present city dates, and from which all later reckoning is taken. London at that day (1666) was for the most part timber-built, and the flames swept unobstructed over an area very nearly approximating that formerly enclosed by London wall.

The Tower escaped; so did All-Hallows, Barking, Crosby Hall, and Austin Friars, but the fire was only checked on the west just before it reached the Temple Church and St. Dunstan's-in-the-West.

He who would know London well must be a pedestrian. Gay, who wrote one of the most exact and lively pictures of the external London of his time, has put it thus:

> " Let others in the jolting coach confide,
> Or in a leaky boat the Thames divide,
> Or box'd within the chair, contemn the street,
> And trust their safety to another's feet:
> Still let me walk."

Such characteristic features as are properly applicable to the Thames have been dealt with in the chapter devoted thereto. With other localities and natural features it is hardly possible to more than make mention of the most remarkable.

From Tower Hill to Hampstead Heath, and from the heights of Sydenham to Highgate is embraced the chief of those places which are continually referred to in the written or spoken word on London. The Fleet and its ditch, with their unsavoury reputations, have been filled up. The Regent's Canal, which enters the Thames below Wapping, winds its way, now above ground and occasionally beneath, as a sort of northern boundary of London proper. Of other waterways, there are none on the north, while on the south there are but two minor streams, Beverly Brook and the River Wandle, which flow sluggishly from the Surrey downs into the Thames near Westminster.

As for elevations, the greatest are the four cardinal points before mentioned.

Tower Hill, with its rather ghastly romance, is first and foremost in the minds of the native and visitor alike. This particular locality has changed but little, if at all, since Dickens' day. The Minories, the Mint, Trinity House, the embattled " Tower " itself, with the central greensward enclosed by iron railings, and the great warehouses of St. Katherine's Dock, all remain as they must have been for years. The only new thing which has come into view is the garish and insincere Tower Bridge, undeniably fine as to its general effect when viewed from a distance down-river, with its historic background and the busy activities of the river at its feet. A sentiment which is speedily dispelled when one realizes that it is but a mere granite shell hung together by invisible iron girders. Something of the solidity of the Tower and the sincerity of a former day is lacking, which can but result in a natural contempt for the utilitarianism which sacrifices the true art expres⁻ion in a city's monuments.

Of the great breathing-places of London, Hyde Park ranks easily the first, with Regent's Park, the Green Park, St. James' Park, Battersea Park, and Victoria Park in the order named. The famous Heath of Hampstead and Richmond Park should be included, but they are treated of elsewhere.

Hyde Park as an institution dates from the sixteenth century. and with Kensington Gardens — that portion which adjoins Kensington Palace — has undergone no great changes during the past hundred years.

At Hyde Park Corner is the famous Apsley House presented by the nation to the Duke of Wellington. At Cumberland Gate was Tyburn. The "Ring" near Grosvenor Gate was the scene of gallantries of the days of Charles II.; of late it has been devoted to the games of gamins and street urchins. The Serpentine is a rather suggestively and incongruously named serpentine body of water,

THE DUKE OF WELLINGTON'S FUNERAL PASSING APSLEY HOUSE.

which in a way serves to give a variety to an otherwise somewhat monotonous prospect.

The first Great International Exhibition was held in Hyde Park in 1851, and rank and fashion, in the mid-Victorian era, " church paraded " in a somewhat more exclusive manner than pursued by the participants in the present vulgar show. The Green Park and St. James's Park touch each other at the angles and, in a way, may be considered as a part of one general plan, though for a fact they vary somewhat as to their characteristics and functions, though under the same " Ranger," a functionary whose office is one of those sinecures which under a long-suffering, tax-burdened public are still permitted to abound.

The history of Regent's Park, London's other great open space, is brief. In 1812, the year of Dickens' birth, a writer called it " one of the most fashionable Sunday promenades about town." It certainly appears to have been quite as much the vogue for promenading as Hyde Park, though the latter retained its supremacy as a driving and riding place. The Zoological Gardens, founded in 1826, here situated, possess a perennial interest for young and old. The principal founders were Sir Humphrey Davy and Sir Stamford Raffles.

The rambler in old London, whether he be on

foot or in a cab, or by the more humble and not inconvenient "'bus," will, if he be in the proper spirit for that edifying occupation, be duly impressed by the mile-stones with which the main roads are set. Along the historic " Bath Road," the " Great North Road," the " Portsmouth Road," or the " Dover Road," throughout their entire length, are those silent though expressive monuments to the city's greatness.

In old coaching days the custom was perhaps more of a consolation than it proves to-day, and whether the Londoner was on pleasure bent, to the Derby or Epsom, or coaching it to Ipswich or Rochester, — as did Pickwick, — the mile-stones were always a cheerful link between two extremes.

To-day their functions are no less active; the advent of the bicycle and the motor-car makes it more necessary than ever that they should be there to mark distance and direction.

No more humourous aspect has ever been remarked than the anecdote recounted by a nineteenth-century historian of the hunt of one Jedediah Jones for the imaginary or long since departed " Hicks' Hall," from which the mile-stones, cryptogrammatically, stated that " this stone was ten (nine, eight, etc.) miles from Hicks' Hall." The individual in question never was able to find the mythical "Hicks' Hall," nor the equally vague "Standard in Cornhill," the latter being referred to by an accommodating 'bus driver in this wise: "Put ye down at the 'Standard in Cornhill?'— that's a good one! I should like to know who ever seed the 'Standard in Cornhill.' Ve knows the 'Svan wi' Two Necks' and the 'Vite Horse' in Piccadilly, but I never heerd of anybody that ever seed the 'Standard in Cornhill.' Ve simply reckons by it."

The suburbs of London in Dickens' time were full of such puzzling mile-stones. As late as 1831 a gate existed at Tyburn turnpike, and so, as if marking the distinction between London and the country, the mile-stones read from Tyburn.

Hyde Park Corner is still used in a similar way. Other stones read merely from London, but, as it would be difficult to know what part of London might best be taken to suit the purposes of the majority, the statement seems as vague as was Hicks' Hall. Why not, as a writer of the day expressed it, measure from the G. P. O.? which to the stranger might prove quite as unintelligible, meaning in this case, however, General Post-Office.

The population return of 1831 shows a plan with a circle drawn eight miles from the centre, a region which then comprised 1,776,000 inhabitants. By

1841 the circle was reduced to a radius of one-half, and the population was still as great as that contained in the larger circle of a decade before. Thus the history of the growth of London shows that its greatest activities came with the beginning of the Victorian era.

By the census of 1861, the population of the City — the E. C. District — was only 112,247; while including that with the entire metropolis, the number was 2,803,034, or *twenty-five times* as great as the former. It may here be remarked that the non-resident, or, more properly, "non-sleeping" population of the City is becoming larger every year, on account of the substitution of public buildings, railway stations and viaducts, and large warehouses, in place of ordinary dwelling-houses. Fewer and fewer people *live* in the City. In 1851, the number was 127,869; it lessened by more than 15,000 between that year and 1861; while the population of the *whole* metropolis increased by as many as 440,-000 in the same space of time.

In 1870, when Dickens was still living, the whole population was computed at 3,251,804, and the E. C. population was further reduced to 74,732.

In 1901 the "City" contained only 3,900 inhabited houses, and but 27,664 persons composed the night population.

The territorial limits or extent of London must vary greatly according as to whether one refers to "The City," "London proper," or "Greater London," a phrase which is generally understood of the people as comprehending not only the contiguous suburbs of a city, but those residential communities closely allied thereto, and drawing, as it were, their support from it. If the latter, there seems no reason why London might not well be thought to include pretty much all of Kent and Surrey, — the home counties lying immediately south of the Thames, — though in reality one very soon gets into green fields in this direction, and but for the ominous signs of the builder and the enigmatic references of the native to the "city" or "town," the stranger, at least, might think himself actually far from the madding throng.

For a fact this is not so, and local life centres, even now, as it did in days gone by, very much around the happenings of the day in London itself.

Taking it in its most restricted and confined literal sense, a circuit of London cannot be better expressed than by quoting the following passage from an author who wrote during the early Victorian period.

"I heard him relate that he had the curiosity to measure the circuit of London by a perambulation thereof. The account he gave was to this effect: He set out from his house in the Strand toward Chelsea, and, having reached the bridge beyond the water works, Battersea, he directed his course to Marylebone, from whence, pursuing an eastern direction, he skirted the town and crossed the Islington road at the 'Angel.' . . . passing through Hoxton he got to Shoreditch, thence to Bethnal Green, and from thence to Stepney, where he recruited his steps with a glass of brandy. From Stepney he passed on to Limehouse, and took into his route the adjacent hamlet of Poplar, when he became sensible that to complete his design he must take in Southwark. This put him to a stand, but he soon determined on his course, for, taking a boat, he landed at the Red House at Deptford and made his way to Saye's Court, where the wet dock is, and, keeping the houses along Rotherhithe to the right, he got to Bermondsey, thence by the south end of Kent Road to Newington, and over St. George's Fields to Lambeth, and crossing over at Millbank, continued his way to Charing Cross and along the Strand to Norfolk Street, from whence he had set out. The whole excursion took him from nine in the morning to three in the afternoon, and, according to his rate of walking, he computed the circuit of London at about twenty miles."

Since this was written, even these areas have probably extended considerably, until to-day the circuit is more nearly fifty miles than twenty, but in assuming that such an itinerary of twenty miles covers the ground specifically mentioned, it holds equally true to-day that this would be a stroll which would exhibit most of the distinguishing features and characteristics of the city.

Modes of conveyance have been improved. One finds the plebeian cab or "growler," the more fastidious hansom, and the popular electric tram, which is fast replacing the omnibus in the outlying portions, to say nothing of the underground railways now being "electrified," as the management put it.

These improvements have made not only distances seem less great, but have done much toward the speedy getting about from one place to another.

It matters not how the visitor enters London; he is bound to be duly impressed by the immensity of it. In olden times the ambassador to St. James' was met at Dover, where he first set foot upon English soil, by the Governor of the Castle and the local Mayor. From here he was passed on in state to the great cathedral city of Canterbury, sojourned for a space beneath the shadow of Rochester Castle, crossed the Medway, and finally reached Gravesend, reckoned the entry to the port of London. Here he was received by the Lord Mayor of London and the Lord Chamberlain, and "took to water in the royal galley-foist," or barge, when he was rowed toward London by the Royal Watermen, an institution of sturdy fellows which has survived to this day, even appearing occasionally in their picturesque costumes at some river fête or function at Windsor.

With a modern visitor it is somewhat different; he usually enters by one of the eight great gateways, London Bridge, Waterloo, Euston, Paddington, St. Pancras, King's Cross, Victoria or Charing Cross, unless by any chance he arrives by sea, which is seldom; the port of London, for the great ocean liner, is mostly a "home port," usually embarking or disembarking passengers at some place on the south or west coast, — Southampton, Plymouth, Liverpool, or Glasgow.

In either case, he is ushered instantly into a great, seething world, unlike, in many of its features, anything elsewhere, with its seemingly inextricable maze of streets and bustle of carriages, omnibuses, and foot-passengers.

He sees the noble dome of St. Paul's rising over all, possibly the massiveness of the Tower, or the twin towers of Westminster, of those of the "New Houses of Parliament," as they are still referred to.

From the south only, however, does the traveller

obtain a really pleasing first impression. Here in crossing any one of the five central bridges he comes at once upon a prospect which is truly grand.

The true pilgrim — he who visits a shrine for the love of its patron — is the one individual who gets the best of life and incidentally of travel. London sightseeing appeals largely to the American, and it is to him that most of the sights and scenes of the London of to-day — and for that matter, of the past fifty years — most appeal. In the reign of James I. sights, of a sort, were even then patronized, presumably by the stranger. "The Londoner never goes anywhere or sees anything," as one has put it. In those days it cost two pence to ascend to the top of Old St. Paul's, and in the Georges' time, a penny to ascend the "Monument." To-day this latter treat costs three pence, which is probably an indication of the tendency of the times to raise prices.

With many it may be said it is merely a rush and a scramble, "personally conducted," or otherwise, to get over as large a space of ground in a given time as legs and lungs will carry one. Walpole remarked the same sad state of affairs when he wrote of the Houghton visitors.

"They come and ask what such a room is called . . . write it down; admire a cabbage or a lobster in a market piece (picture?) ; dispute as to whether the last room was green or purple, and then hurry to the inn for fear the fish should be overdressed."

One who knows his London is amused at the disappointment that the visitor often feels when comparing his impression of London, as it really is, with the London of his imagination.

As they ride down Fleet Street they are surprised at the meanness of the buildings as compared with those which had existed in their mind's eye. This might not be the case were but their eyes directed to the right quarter. Often and often one has seen the stranger on a 'bus gazing at the houses in Fleet Street instead of looking, as he should, right ahead. In this way he misses the most sublime views in London : that of the " Highway of Letters " in its true relation to St. Paul's in the east and the Abbey in the west.

The long dip of the street and the opposite hill of Ludgate give an incomparable majesty to the Cathedral, crowning the populous hill, soaring serenely above the vista of houses, gables, chimneys. signals, and telegraph wires. —

> " Above the smoke and stir of this dim spot,
>   Which men call town."

Coming by one of the existing modern gateways the railway termini, before mentioned, the visitor would be well advised to reënter London the next day *via* the " Uxbridge Road," upon an omnibus bound for the Bank, securing a front seat. He will then make his triumphal entry along five miles of straight roadway, flanked by magnificent streets, parks, and shops, until, crossing Holborn Viaduct, he is borne past the General Post-Office, under the shadow of St. Paul's, and along Cheapside to the portico of the Royal Exchange — the hub of the world. As Byron well knew, only time reveals London:

> " The man who has stood on the Acropolis
> And looked down over Attica; or he
> Who has sailed where picturesque Constantinople is,
> Or seen Timbuctoo, or hath taken tea
> In small-eyed China's crockery-ware metropolis,
> Or sat midst the bricks of Nineveh,
> May not think much of London's first appearance;
> *But ask him what he thinks of it a year hence !* "

As with society, so with certain localities of London; there are some features which need not be described; indeed they are not fit to be, and, while it cannot be said that Dickens ever expressed himself in manner aught but proper, there are details of the lives and haunts of the lower classes of which a discussion to any extent should be reserved for those economic works which treat solely of social questions. The " Hell's Kitchens " and " Devil's

Furnaces," all are found in most every large city
of Europe and America; and it cannot be said that
the state of affairs, with regard thereto, is in any
way improving, though an occasional slum is blotted
out entirely.

Not alone from a false, or a prudish, refinement
are these questions kept in the background, but more
particularly are they diminished in view in order
to confine the contents of this book to a résumé of
the facts which are the most agreeable. Even in
those localities where there is little else but crime
and ignorance, suffering and sorrow, there is also,
in some measure, propriety and elegance, comfort
and pleasure.

If the old " Tabard " of Chaucer's day has given
way to a garish and execrable modern " Public
House," some of the sentiment still hangs over the
locality, and so, too, with the riverside communities
of Limehouse and Wapping. Sentiment as well
as other emotions are unmistakably reminiscent,
and the enthusiastic admirer of Dickens, none the
less than the general lover of a historical past, will
derive much pleasure from tracing itineraries for
himself among the former sites and scenes of the
time, not far gone, of which he wrote.

Eastcheap has lost some of its old-world atmosphere, and is now given over to the coster element.

Finsbury and Islington are covered with long rows of dull-looking houses which have existed for a matter of fifty or seventy-five years, with but little change except an occasional new shop-front and a new street cut through here and there. Spring Gardens, near Trafalgar Square, is no longer a garden, and is as dull and gloomy a place as any flagged courtyard in a less aristocratic neighbourhood.

The old " Fleet Ditch " no longer runs its course across Holborn and into the Thames at Blackfriars. Churches, palaces, theatres, prisons, and even hospitals have, in a measure, given way to progressive change and improvement.

Guy's Hospital, identified with letters from the very foundation of its patron, — one Thomas Guy, a bookseller of Lombard Street, — dates only from the eighteenth century, and has to-day changed little from what it was in Dickens' time, when he lived in near-by Lant Street, and the fictional character of " Sawyer " gave his famous party to which " Mr. Pickwick " was invited. " It's near Guy's," said Sawyer, " and handy for me, you know."

On the whole, London is remarkably well preserved; its great aspects suffer but very little change, and the landmarks and monuments which met Dickens' gaze are sufficiently numerous and splendid to still be recognizable by any who possess any degree of familiarity with his life and works. Many well-known topographical features are still to be found within the sound of Bow Bells and Westminster. Those of the Strand and Fleet Street, of the Borough, Bermondsey, Southwark southward of the river, and Bloomsbury in the north, form that debatable ground which is ever busy with hurrying feet. The street-sweeper, though, has mostly disappeared, and the pavements of Whitehall are more evenly laid than were the Halls of Hampton Court in Wolsey's day.

Where streets run off from the great thoroughfares, they are often narrow and in a way ill kept, but this is due more to their confined area than to any carelessness or predisposition on the part of the authorities to ignore cleanliness.

London possesses a series of topographical divisions peculiar to itself, when one considers the number thereof, referring to the numerous squares which, in a way, correspond to the Continental place, platz, or plaza. It is, however, a thing quite different. It may be a residential square, like Bedford, Bloomsbury, or Belgrave Squares, or, like Covent Garden and Lincoln's Inn Fields, given over to business of a certain sedate kind. These latter two are the oldest of London squares. Or, like Trafalgar Square, of a frankly commercial aspect.

On the Continent they are generally more of architectural pretensions than in London, and their functions are quite different, having more of a public or ceremonial character; whereas here the more exclusive are surrounded with the houses of the nobility or aristocracy, or what passes for it in these days; or, as in the case of Trafalgar Square, — in itself of splendid architectural value, — little more than a point of crossing or meeting of streets, like Piccadilly and Oxford Circus.

In the " City," the open spaces are of great historical association; namely, Charterhouse, Bridgewater, Salisbury, Gough, and Warwick Squares. They show very few signs of life and humanity of a Sunday or a holiday, but are active enough at other times.

Further west are the quiet precincts of the Temple and Lincoln's Inn Fields, one of the most ancient and, on the whole, the most attractive of all, with its famous houses and institutions of a storied past.

While, if not actually to be counted as city squares, they perform in no small degree many of their functions.

Red Lion Square, to the north of Fleet Street, is

gloomy enough, and reminiscent of the old "Red Lion" Inn, for long "the largest and best frequented inn in Holborn," and yet more worthily, as being the residence of Milton after his pardon from King Charles.

Soho Square and Golden Square are quiet and charming retreats, away from the bustle of the shoppers of Regent and Oxford Streets, though perhaps melancholy enough to the seeker after real architectural charm and beauty.

It is to Bloomsbury that the heart of the American most fondly turns, whether he takes residence there by reason of its being "so near to the British Museum, you know," or for motives of economy, either of which should be sufficient of itself, likewise commendable.

The museum itself, with its reading-room and collections, is the great attraction, it cannot be denied, of this section of London, and Bloomsbury Square, Torrington Square, Queen's Square, and Mecklenburgh Square, where Dickens lived and wrote much of "Pickwick" in 1837-39, are given over largely to "board-residence" establishments for the visitor, or he who for reasons good and true desires to make his abode in historic old Bloomsbury.

In Dickens' time the region had become the

haunt of those who affected science, literature, or art, by reason of the proximity of the British Museum and the newly founded University of London.

The wealthy element, who were not desirous of being classed among the fashionables, were attracted here by its nearness to the open country and Regent's Park. Thus, clustering around Bloomsbury is a whole nucleus of squares; "some comely," says a writer, "some elegant," and all with a middle-class air about them.

Still further west are the aristocratic and exclusive St. James' Square, Berkley, Belgrave, Grosvenor, Manchester, Devonshire, and many more rectangles which are still the possession of the exclusives and pseudo-fashionables. Their histories and their goings-on are lengthy chronicles, and are not within the purpose of this book, hence may be dismissed with mere mention.

The flow of the Thames from west to east through the metropolis has given a general direction to the lines of street; the principal thoroughfares being, in some measure, parallel to the river, with the inferior, or at least shorter, streets branching from them. Intersecting the town lengthwise, or from east to west, are two great leading thoroughfares at a short distance from each other, but gradually diverging at their western extremity.

One of these routes begins in the eastern environs,
near Blackwall, and extends along Whitechapel,
Leadenhall Street, Cornhill, the Poultry, Cheapside,
Newgate Street, Holborn, and Oxford Street. The
other may be considered as starting at London
Bridge, and passing up King William Street into
Cheapside, at the western end of which it makes
a bend round St. Paul's Churchyard; thence proceeds down Ludgate Hill, along Fleet Street and
the Strand to Charing Cross, where it sends a
branch off to the left to Whitehall, and another
diagonally to the right, up Cockspur Street; this
leads forward into Pall Mall, and sends an offshoot
up Waterloo Place into Piccadilly, which proceeds
westward to Hyde Park Corner. These are the
two main lines of the metropolis.

Of recent years two important new thoroughfares
have been made, viz., New Cannon Street, extending from London Bridge to St. Paul's Churchyard,
and Queen Victoria Street, which, leaving the Mansion House, crosses Cannon Street about its centre,
and extends to Blackfriars Bridge. The third main
route begins at the Bank, and passes through the
City Road and the New Road to Paddington and
Westbourne. The New Road here mentioned has
been renamed in three sections, — Pentonville Road,
from Islington to King's Cross; Euston Road, from

King's Cross to Regent's Park; and Marylebone Road, from Regent's Park to Paddington. The main cross-branches in the metropolis are Farringdon Street, leading from Blackfriars Bridge to Holborn, and thence to King's Cross; the Haymarket, leading from Cockspur Street; and Regent Street, running northwesterly in the direction of Regent's Park. Others from the north of Holborn are Tottenham Court Road, parallel to Gower Street, where the Dickenses first lived when they came to London. Gray's Inn Road, near which is Gray's Inn, where Dickens himself was employed as a lawyer's clerk, and Doughty Street, where, at No. 48, can still be seen Dickens' house, as a signboard on the door announces: " Dickens lived here in 1837." Aldersgate, continued as Goswell Road, connects with Islington and Whitechapel, and Mile End Road leads to Essex.

Such were the few main arteries of traffic in Dickens' day, and even unto the present; the complaint has been that there are not more direct thoroughfares of a suitable width, both lengthwise and crosswise, to cope with the immense and cumbersome traffic of 'bus and dray, to say nothing of carts and cabs.

Nothing is likely to give the stranger a just estimate of the magnitude of this more than will the observance of the excellent police control of the cross traffic, when, in some measure, its volume will be apparent.

It would perhaps be impossible in a work such as this that any one locality could be described with anything like adequate completeness. Certainly one would not hope to cover the ground entire, where every division and subdivision partakes severally of widely different characteristics.

Southwark and the Borough, with its High Street, St. George's Church and Fields, the old Marshalsea — or the memory of it — " The King's Bench " Prison, and " Guy's," are something quite different with respect to manners and customs from Whitechapel or Limehouse.

So, too, are St. Giles' and Pimlico in the west, and Hampstead and Highgate in North London. Since all of these are dealt with elsewhere, to a greater or lesser degree, a few comments on the Whitechapel of Dickens' day must suffice here, and, truth to tell, it has not greatly changed since that time, save for a periodical cleaning up and broadening of the main thoroughfare. It is with more or less contempt and disgust that Whitechapel is commonly recalled to mind. Still, Whitechapel is neither more nor less disreputable than many other localities sustained by a similar strata of society. It serves, however, to illustrate the life of the east end, as contrasted with that of the west of London — the other pole of the social sphere — and is, moreover, peopled by that class which Dickens, in a large measure, incorporated into the novels.

In ancient times Northumberland, Throgmorton, and Crosby were noble names associated therewith. In Dickens' day butchers, it would seem, were the predominate species of humanity, while to-day Jewish " sweat-shops " are in the ascendant, a sufficiently fine distinction to render it recognizable to any dweller in a large city, whatever his nationality.

The fleur-de-lis and royal blazonings are no longer seen, and such good old Anglo-Saxon names as Stiles, Stiggins, and Stodges are effectually obliterated from shop signs. How changed this ancient neighbourhood is from what it must once have been! Crosby Hall, in Bishopsgate Street, not far distant, the *ci-devant* palace of Richard II., is now a mere eating-house, albeit a very good one. And as for the other noble houses, they have gone the way of all fanes when once encroached upon by the demands of business progress.

Baynard Castle, where Henry VII. received his ambassadors, and in which the crafty Cecil plotted against Lady Jane Grey, almost before the ink was dry with which he had solemnly registered his name to serve her, has long ago been numbered amongst the things that were. The archers of Mile-end, with their chains of gold, have departed: the spot on which the tent stood, where bluff Hal regaled himself after having witnessed their sports, is now covered with mean-looking houses: as one has said, " the poetry of ancient London is well-nigh dead."

The voice of the stream is for ever hushed that went murmuring before the dwellings of our forefathers, along Aldgate and down Fenchurch Street, and past the door of Sir Thomas Gresham's house, in Lombard Street, until it doubled round by the Mansion House and emptied itself into the river. There is still the sound of rushing waters by the Steam-Packet Wharf, at London Bridge; but how different to the "brawling brook" of former days is the "evil odour" which arises from the poisonous sewers of to-day.

And to what have these old-world splendours given place? Splendid gin-shops, plate-glass palaces, into which squalor and misery rush and drown the remembrance of their wretchedness in drowsy and poisonous potations of an inferior quality of liquor. Such splendour and squalor is the very contrast which makes thinking men pause, and pause again.

WHITECHAPEL.

The Whitechapel butcher was of the old school.
He delighted in a blue livery, and wore his "steel"
with as much satisfaction as a young ensign does
his sword. He neither spurned the worsted leggins
nor duck apron; but with bare muscular arms, and
knife keen enough to sever the hamstring of a bull,
took his stand proudly at the front of his shop, and
looked "lovingly" on the well-fed joints above
his head. The gutters before his door literally ran
with blood: pass by whenever you would, there
the crimson current constantly flowed; and the
smell the passenger inhaled was not that of "Ar-
aby." A "Whitechapel bird" and a "Whitechapel
butcher" were once synonymous phrases, used to
denote a character the very reverse of a gentleman;
but, says a writer of the fifties, "in the manners
of the latter we believe there is a great improvement, and that more than one 'knight of the cleaver'
who here in the daytime manufacture sheep into
mutton chops, keeps his country house."

The viands offered for sale augur well for the
strength of the stomachs of the Whitechapel popu-
lace. The sheeps' trotters look as if they had
scarcely had time enough to kick off the dirt before
they were potted; and as for the ham, it appears
bleached, instead of salted; and to look at the sand-
wiches, you would think they were anything except

what they are called. As for the fried fish, it resembles coarse red sand-paper; and you would sooner think of purchasing a penny-worth to polish the handle of a cricket bat or racket, than of trying its qualities in any other way. The "black puddings" resemble great fossil ammonites, cut up lengthwise. What the "faggots" are made of, which form such a popular dish in this neighbourhood, we have yet to learn. We have heard rumours of chopped lights, liver, suet, and onions as being the components of these dusky dainties; but he must be a daring man who would convince himself by tasting: for our part, it would seem that there was a great mystery to be unravelled before the innumerable strata which form these smoking hillocks will ever be made known. The pork pies which you see in these windows contain no such effeminate morsels as lean meat, but have the appearance of good substantial bladders of lard shoved into a strong crust, and "done brown" in a superheated oven.

Such, crudely, is an impression of certain aspects of "trade" in Whitechapel, but its most characteristic feature outside of the innumerable hawkers of nearly everything under the sun, new or old, which can be sold at a relatively low price, is the famous "Rag Fair," a sort of "old clo's" mart,

whose presiding geniuses are invariably of the Jewish persuasion, either male or female. Rags which
may have clothed the fair person of a duchess have
here so fallen as to be fit only for dusting cloths.
The insistent vender will assure you that they have
been worn but "werry leetle, werry leetle, indeed.
. . . Vell, vot of it, look at the pryshe!"

Dank and fetid boxes and barrows, to say naught
of the more ambitious shops, fill the Whitechapel
Road and Petticoat Lane (now changed to Middlesex Street, but some measure of the old activities
may still be seen of a Sunday morning).

A rummaging around will bring to light, likely
enough, something that may once have been a court
dress, a bridal costume, or a ball gown; a pair
of small satin slippers, once white; a rusty crêpe,
a "topper of a manifestly early vintage, or what
not, all may be found here. One might almost fancy
that Pride, in some material personification, might
indeed be found buried beneath the mass of dross,
or having shuffled off its last vestiges of respecta-
bility, its corse might at least be found to have left
its shroud behind; and such these tattered habili-
ments really are. Rag Fair to-day is still the great
graveyard of Fashion; the last cemetery to which
cast-off clothes are borne before they enter upon

another state of existence, and are spirited into dusters and dish-clouts.

Of all modern cities, London, perhaps more than any other, is justly celebrated for the number and variety of its suburbs.

On the northwest are Hampstead, with its noble Heath reminiscent of "highwaymen and scoundrels," and its charming variety of landscape scenery; and Harrow, with its famous old school, associated with the memory of Byron, Peel, and many other eminent men, to the churchyard of which Byron was a frequent visitor. "There is," he wrote to a friend in after years, "a spot in the churchyard, near the footpath on the brow of the hill looking toward Windsor, and a tomb (bearing the name of Peachey) under a large tree, where I used to sit for hours and hours when a boy." Nearly northward are Highgate, with its fringe of woods, and its remarkable series of ponds; Finchley, also once celebrated for its highwaymen, but now for its cemeteries; Hornsey, with its ivy-clad church, and its pretty winding New River; and Barnet, with its great annual fair, still an institution attended largely by costers and horse-traders. On the northeast are Edmonton, with its tavern, which the readers of "John Gilpin" will of course never forget; Enfield, where the government manufactures rifles on a vast scale; Waltham, notable for its ancient abbey church; and Epping Forest, a boon to picnic parties from the east end of London.

South of the Thames, likewise, there are many pretty spots, quite distinct from those which border upon the river's bank. Wimbledon, with its furze-clad common and picturesque windmill; Mitcham, with its herb gardens; Norwood, a pleasant bit of high ground, from which a view of London from the south can be had; Lewisham and Bromley, surrounded by many pretty bits of scenery; Black-heath, a famous place for golf and other outdoor games; Eltham, where a bit of King John's palace is still left to view; the Crays, a string of pictur-esque villages on the banks of the River Cray, etc. Dulwich is a village about five miles south of Lon-don Bridge. Here Edward Alleyn, or Allen, a dis-tinguished actor in the reign of James I., founded and endowed an hospital or college, called Dulwich College, for the residence and support of poor per-sons, under certain limitations.

THE END.

A BRIEF CHRONOLOGY OF SOME OF THE MORE IMPORTANT EVENTS IN THE HISTORY OF THE CITY OF LONDON DURING THE LIFETIME OF CHARLES DICKENS.

1812 Oct. 10. Present Drury Lane Theatre opened.

1814 Nov. 29. The Times newspaper first printed by steam.

1816 Vauxhall Bridge opened.

1817 Waterloo Bridge opened.

1818 Furnival's Inn rebuilt.

1820 Jan. 29. George III. died.
Cabs came in.

1821 Bank of England completed by Sir John Soane.

1824 March 15. First pile of London Bridge driven.
First stone of new Post-office laid.
May 10. National Gallery first opened.

1825 Thames Tunnel commenced.
Toll-house at Hyde Park Corner removed.

1828 St. Katherine Docks opened.
Birdcage Walk made a public way.

1829 King's College in the Strand commenced.
New police service established by Sir Robert Peel.

1830 June 26. George IV. died.
Omnibuses first introduced by Shillaber; the first ran between Paddington and the Bank.
Covent Garden Market rebuilt.

1831 Hungerford Market commenced.
The Hay Market in Pall Mall removed to Regent's Park.
Exeter Hall opened.

1834 Houses of Parliament burned down.

1835 Duke of York's Column completed.

1837 William IV. died. Accession of Queen Victoria.
Buckingham Palace first occupied.

1838 First Royal Academy Exhibition in Tralfagar Square.

1841 Great Fire at the Tower of London.

1843 Nelson Column placed in Trafalgar Square.

1845 Hungerford Bridge opened.
Lincoln's Inn New Hall opened by Queen Victoria.

1847   Covent Garden Theatre opened as Italian Opera House.

New House of Lords opened.

New Portico and Hall of British Museum opened.

1848   April 10. Great Chartist Demonstration.

1851   Great Exhibition in Hyde Park.

1852   Nov. 18. Duke of Wellington's Funeral.

1855   April 19. Visit of Emperor and Empress of French.

Nov. 30. Visit of King of Sardinia.

1858   Jan. 31. Steamship "Great Eastern" launched.

1860   Underground Railway begun.

1862   March 12. Mr. George Peabody, the American merchant, gives £150,000 to ameliorate the condition of London poor.

May 1. Second International Exhibition opened.

1863   Jan. 10. Underground Railway opened.

March 7. Princess Alexandra, of Denmark, enters London.

1864   Jan. 1. New street opened between Blackfriars' and London Bridge.

Feb. 29. First block of Peabody Buildings opened in Spitalfields.

April 21. Garibaldi receives the freedom of the city.

1866   Jan. 29. Mr. Peabody adds £100,000 to his gift to the London poor.

May 10. Black Friday, commercial panic.

July 24. Riots in Hyde Park.

Sept. 1. Cannon Street Railway Station opened.

1867   Jan. 15. Severe frost; forty lives lost by the breaking of the ice in Regent's Park.

June 3. First stone of Holborn Viaduct laid.

1868   May 13. The Queen lays foundation of St. Thomas' Hospital.

Dec. 5. George Peabody gives another £100,000 to the poor of London.

1869   July 23. Statue of George Peabody unveiled by the Prince of Wales.

Nov. 7. Opening of Holborn Viaduct by the Queen.

1870   July 13. Opening of the Victoria Embankment by the Prince of Wales.

Index

Printed in the United States
138375LV00001B/220/P

9 781409 712572